theatre & prison

Theatre&
Series Editors: Jen Harvie and Dan Rebellato

Published
Colette Conroy: *Theatre & the Body*
Jill Dolan: *Theatre & Sexuality*
Helen Freshwater: *Theatre & Audience*
Jen Harvie: *Theatre & the City*
Nadine Holdsworth: *Theatre & Nation*
Erin Hurley: *Theatre & Feeling*
Joe Kelleher: *Theatre & Politics*
Ric Knowles: *Theatre & Interculturalism*
Caoimhe McAvinchey: *Theatre & Prison*
Helen Nicholson: *Theatre & Education*
Lionel Pilkington: *Theatre & Ireland*
Paul Rae: *Theatre & Human Rights*
Dan Rebellato: *Theatre & Globalization*
Nicholas Ridout: *Theatre & Ethics*

Forthcoming
Susan Bennett: *Theatre & Museums*
Dominic Johnson: *Theatre & the Visual*
Bruce McConachie: *Theatre & the Mind*
Juliet Rufford: *Theatre & Architecture*
Rebecca Schneider: *Theatre & History*

Theatre&
Series Standing Order: ISBN 978–0–230–20327–3 paperback

You can receive further titles in this series as they are published by placing a standing order. Please contact your bookseller or, in the case of difficulty, write to us at the address below with your name and address, the title of the series, and the ISBN quoted above.

Customer Services Department, Palgrave Macmillan Ltd.
Houndmills, Basingstoke, Hampshire, RG21 6XS, England

theatre &
prison

Caoimhe McAvinchey

palgrave
macmillan

First published 2011 by
PALGRAVE MACMILLAN

Palgrave Macmillan in the UK is an imprint of Macmillan Publishers Limited, registered in England, company number 785998, of Houndmills, Basingstoke, Hampshire RG21 6XS.

Palgrave Macmillan in the US is a division of St Martin's Press LLC, 175 Fifth Avenue, New York, NY 10010.

Palgrave Macmillan is the global academic imprint of the above companies and has companies and representatives throughout the world.

Palgrave® and Macmillan® are registered trademarks in the United States, the United Kingdom, Europe and other countries.

ISBN-13: 978–0–230–24793–2 paperback

This book is printed on paper suitable for recycling and made from fully managed and sustained forest sources. Logging, pulping and manufacturing processes are expected to conform to the environmental regulations of the country of origin.

A catalogue record for this book is available from the British Library.

A catalog record for this book is available from the Library of Congress.

10 9 8 7 6 5 4 3 2 1
20 19 18 17 16 15 14 13 12 11

Printed in China

contents

series editors' preface

The theatre is everywhere, from entertainment districts to the fringes, from the rituals of government to the ceremony of the courtroom, from the spectacle of the sporting arena to the theatres of war. Across these many forms stretches a theatrical continuum through which cultures both assert and question themselves.

Theatre has been around for thousands of years, and the ways we study it have changed decisively. It's no longer enough to limit our attention to the canon of Western dramatic literature. Theatre has taken its place within a broad spectrum of performance, connecting it with the wider forces of ritual and revolt that thread through so many spheres of human culture. In turn, this has helped make connections across disciplines; over the past fifty years, theatre and performance have been deployed as key metaphors and practices with which to rethink gender, economics, war, language, the fine arts, culture and one's sense of self.

Theatre & is a long series of short books which hopes to capture the restless interdisciplinary energy of theatre and performance. Each book explores connections between theatre and some aspect of the wider world, asking how the theatre might illuminate the world and how the world might illuminate the theatre. Each book is written by a leading theatre scholar and represents the cutting edge of critical thinking in the discipline.

We have been mindful, however, that the philosophical and theoretical complexity of much contemporary academic writing can act as a barrier to a wider readership. A key aim for these books is that they should all be readable in one sitting by anyone with a curiosity about the subject. The books are challenging, pugnacious, visionary sometimes and, above all, clear. We hope you enjoy them.

Jen Harvie and Dan Rebellato

foreword

When I was the director of the Theatre in Prisons and Probation (TiPP) Centre I used to drive the company van as I travelled to work in regional prison and probation centres. It had 'TiPP Centre' emblazoned on its side, and occasionally people would ask 'What does TiPP stand for?' If I didn't bottle it and lie, I would try to explain, as succinctly as possible, what the work involved. These were improvised mini versions of what now is called the 'public acceptability test', as I tried to convince people in garage forecourts or motorway service stations why, as far as I was concerned, theatre and prisons did have a logical connection. These attempts were always somewhat embarrassed and far from articulate.

More than fifteen years later, and a long time since I worked in a prison, I've now had the pleasure of reading this excellent book by Caoimhe McAvinchey – and wish it had been available at the time. Not because it provides easy answers about the relationship between theatre and prison, but because it offers a comprehensive analysis of the complexity of their interrelation without denying the contradictions and difficulties of the field. Rather than my reluctant rendition of what developing theatre in prisons might be about, McAvinchey provides a carefully crafted account that will be an invaluable resource to embarrassed practitioners, nervous students and over-confident academics for a long time to come.

In 2008 UK Home Secretary Jack Straw called a halt to a 'stand-up' course run by the arts organisation the Comedy School in Whitemoor Prison after the *Sun* newspaper launched a campaign under the headline 'Are You Having a Laugh?' This led to an edict from the Prison Service that governors should ensure that all activities were 'acceptable, purposeful and meet the public acceptability test'. Projects linked to the arts or theatre seemed to be particularly threatened by this new ruling. Individuals and organisations connected to both the arts and rehabilitation of offenders, however, sprang to the defence of the work – and since then there has been no flurry of specialist companies losing their work or being directly threatened. While I'm not claiming times are easy, theatre and arts projects in prison seem to be somewhat robust in this harsh climate. Interestingly my experience of testing public acceptability when working for TiPP indicated that there was no stereotypical antagonistic response – many people understood immediately how the arts could be a useful, purposeful activity in prisons. Jack Straw perhaps should be reminded that the *Sun* is not synonymous with 'the public' and there are many, frequent and important distinctions.

Prison theatre therefore continues to thrive because prisoners, prison educators, governors and the general public understand that the arts can provide something to institutions and the people who live and work in them. Of course precisely what that is changes according to the context – perhaps an innovative form of drug education in one establishment, a form of life skills training in another or an opening to literacy in another. Or perhaps just the sheer pleasure of participating in the arts – something that many governors realise is vital to an environment that knows its duty is to look after prisoners *with humanity and help them lead law-abiding and useful lives in custody and after release* (the Prison Service mission statement). What McAvinchey's timely book does with such skill is place these different demands into a historical and theoretical context, examining how theatre *in* prisons can best be understood in relation to the performance demands of punishment itself and the wider thematic interest in incarceration demonstrated by theatre makers and writers. The book is therefore not a written response to the public acceptability test, but a lucid account of why prison and theatre seem to have this intimate relationship – and perhaps an explanation of why Jack Straw might have thought his test was so necessary.

At the University of Manchester colleagues in the TiPP Centre have taught an undergraduate course in prison theatre for a number of years. After one such course a young student explained her enthusiasm for the programme by saying that she did not want to work again in prisons but 'doing the course reminded me why I liked theatre in the first place'. I personally have not worked in prisons for a number of years, but reading McAvinchey's book reminded me of why I liked prison theatre in the first place – and of how service stations and garage forecourts are exactly the sites where we should be happy to explain the importance of this type of work.

James Thompson
James Thompson is Professor of Applied and Social Theatre at the University of Manchester. He set up the TiPP Centre with Paul Heritage in 1992 and was director until 1999. He is currently director of In Place of War, a project that researches and develops performance in sites of armed conflict. His books include Applied Theatre: Bewilderment and Beyond *(2003),* Digging Up Stories: Applied Theatre Performance and War *(2005),* Performance Affects *(2009) and with Jenny Hughes and Michael Balfour* Performance In Place of War *(2009).*

theatre & prison

Introduction

Her Majesty's Prison Wormwood Scrubs is a closed, medium-security men's prison in Acton, West London. Built by convict labour between 1875 and 1891, the prison's architecture articulates the Victorian state's response to crime and punishment in its scale, austerity and opaqueness. In May 2008 I joined a group of more than one hundred people gathered outside the prison gatehouse, a site familiar to many as the entrance to the fictional HMP Slade in the 1970s British sit-com *Porridge*. We were the audience for a production of John Steinbeck's *Of Mice and Men* (Music Box Theatre, New York, 1937) by Only Connect theatre company, performed by a cast of prisoners and professional actors.

A working prison is a very particular venue presenting a different contract to an audience familiar with traditional theatre spaces. To book a ticket for the production, the audience had to contact the theatre company with their passport details. In this venue, there is no cloakroom or bar, and as an audience with no freedom to come and go, you arrive and leave as a group, together.

Inside the gatehouse, prison guards, in a businesslike but not unfriendly way, acted as the front-of-house team, checking passport details against an official list of visitors, inspecting handbags and rucksacks. Security procedures completed, we were ushered across the prison yard towards the chapel, where the production was staged. As we walked we were in full view of one of the prison's wings. Prisoners leaned against their cell windows, watching and calling down to us. We were neither family, friends nor legal representation – the usual kind of visitors; we were a theatre audience who had come to see a play about male friendship and the mercurial qualities of morality and justice.

At the end of the production, the cast members returned to the stage and spoke to the audience about the pleasures and challenges of making this piece of theatre, how it had helped them to see themselves in a way that was not defined solely by the institution they currently lived in and how they were determined not to return to prison after their release. After family members and friends in the audience had congratulated them, the cast were escorted from the theatre back to their cells. The audience was then ushered from the chapel, across the yard, through the gatehouse and out onto the residential streets that surround the prison.

Only Connect's production raises many specific questions: Why would HMP Wormwood Scrubs allow a theatre project to happen within its walls? Why would it agree to this production being open to a public audience? Why would a theatre company choose to work in prison with prisoners? Was the audience turning up to see a production of *Of Mice and Men*? Or a piece of theatre *in* a prison? Or to look at prisoners performing? Or to witness reformation?

I hope that these types of questions, raised by specific instances and examples in this book, will inform more general understandings about the relationship between theatre, performance and prison. By addressing such issues, we can consider how theatre and performance can help us investigate and understand the political, social and economic consequences of the use of prison in the twenty-first century.

Likewise, thinking about prison helps us understand aspects of theatre and performance: how representations of criminal bodies are marked by race, class, sexuality and gender; how recent developments in the funding and methodologies of theatre practice in prison are embroiled in neoliberal narratives that fuel the corrections industry; and how audiences are invited to affectively respond to or critically engage with theatre in or about prison.

Thinking about theatre and prison provokes an inquiry into the relationship between the individual and the state, forcing us to consider how prisons perform within the economy of punishment, and compelling us to question narratives of crime, punishment and justice that are believed to be true and effective. This is the terrain of *Theatre & Prison*.

Why think about the relationship between theatre and prison?

At the beginning of the twenty-first century, we take prisons for granted. As Vivien Stern writes in *A Sin against the Future: Imprisonment in the World*, 'Everyone has them. It is as normal to have prisons as to have schools or hospitals' (1998, p. xx). For those of us who have never been sentenced, or who do not work in or visit prisons, our access to the prison world is mediated by others' representations of it. The idea of prison in the cultural imagination is compelling: it is a hidden world populated by people who have broken the social contract of law and order. These single-sex institutions are, in many cultural representations, invested with homoerotic charge and tension as inmates and staff negotiate contradictory desires of liberty and containment.

Images of incarceration saturate popular culture. Films such as *The Big House* (1930), *Escape from Alcatraz* (1979), *The Shawshank Redemption* (1994) and *Dead Man Walking* (1995) have become iconic representations of life behind bars. Over the past four decades, long-running television series such as *Porridge*, *Prisoner: Cell Block H*, *Bad Girls*, *Prison Break* and *Oz* have drawn regular audiences of millions who tune in for their weekly fix of prison life. Escapes, riots, institutional brutality and redemption are particular narratives characteristic of prison dramas – dramas replete with stock characters: the sadistic guard, the naïve new prisoner, the lovable rascal and the savvy inmate who runs the wing.

On occasion, individual institutions will smash through the representational world of incarceration and remind us of their urgent materiality. The Maze in Northern Ireland was the notorious site of IRA hunger strikes in the early 1980s. In South Africa, under Apartheid, Robben Island held over 3,000 political prisoners who protested against racist policies of segregation. In 1992, HMP Strangeways in Manchester was catapulted to public attention when prisoners held a 25-day riot and roof-top protest against their living conditions. In the same year, Carandiru in São Paulo, Brazil, an enormous prison which held 8,000 prisoners, was the site of a massacre of 111 inmates at the hands of the state's military police. In recent years, the physical, psychological and sexual torture of detainees at the Abu Ghraib and Guantánamo prison camps by US army personnel has provoked international outrage and shame.

Some decommissioned prisons offer an alternative world to that presented in the headlines, one of comfort and entertainment. Hotels in converted prisons, ranging from the luxurious five-star Malmaison in Oxford, England, to the backpackers' hostel in Napier Prison in New Zealand, market themselves on their penal past.

The Clink in London, Alcatraz in San Francisco and the Old Melbourne Gaol have become destinations in the growing area of dark tourism. At The Clink prison museum, businesses looking for an alternative venue for their staff parties can select from a panoply of opportunities in the underground torture chambers, including wine receptions, themed entertainment and 'the opportunity to put your head on an original execution block' (www.clink.co.uk). If The Clink's offer is unappealing, the museum's name does at least do something else: it reminds us that our language is rich with slang terms, terms that have survived many generations, describing the site of incarceration: the clanger, the slammer, the nick, the joint, chokey.

In short, the confluence of film, television drama, news reportage and language gives prison the sheen of familiarity. Prison – both as a place and as a mode of punishment – has permeated our cultural landscape and shaped our expectations of incarceration as an ordinary and accepted part of judicial procedures. In effect, as David Garland notes in *Punishment and Modern Society*, prison's symbolic power, evidenced throughout culture, ensures that it 'is as much a basic metaphor of our cultural imagination as it is a feature of our penal policy' (1990, p. 260).

But the perceived access that these cultural articulations provide is often superficial, telling us little about prison *either* as a material, constructed site (a place where people live and work) *or* as an idea (how societies choose to punish). News stories focus on crises within the existing system – overcrowding, prison gangs, deaths in custody; popular fictional narratives are fuelled by dramatic crises – 'the escape' or 'the abusive guard'. Both tell us about something that has 'gone wrong' in a particular moment. Neither encourages any real critique of prison as a punishment, deterrent or agent of rehabilitation. This entrenched normalcy of cultural representation contributes to a vacuum of public and political debate regarding prison's ideological rationale. Safe in the shared assumption that 'we've always had them', we forget to ask, 'What are they for?'

This book argues that there is an urgent political, economic, social and cultural need for a critical re-engagement with the *idea* of prison and that theatre, although not itself immune from using prison as cultural shorthand, provides us with unique opportunities for this re-engagement. In order to understand how theatre does so, we need to consider the context it addresses.

Imprisonment in the twenty-first century

At the beginning of the twenty-first century, more than 10 million people were incarcerated around the world. Over the past 20 years there has been a steady rise in the prison population in every continent, and statistics reveal that this upward trend shows no sign of abating.

Most countries use the deprivation of liberty as a form of punishment; however, the use and conditions of incarceration vary in different cultural contexts. For example, the USA has the largest prison population in the world, with over 2,300,000 people incarcerated. For every 100,000 people in the overall population, 753 are in prison (International Centre for Prison Studies, *World Prison Brief*, 2010). The USA is also the home of the super-maximum-security prison, or the Supermax. Prisoners considered to represent the highest threat to society are kept in 23–24-hour solitary confinement where every movement is observed via closed-circuit television cameras and human contact is minimal. In this context, prisoners are removed from society with no hope of, or preparation for, being returned to it.

Other countries have a very different approach. Norway has a prison population of just over 3,000 people. Like those of most countries, its rates of incarceration have increased over the past 20 years, but only slightly. For every 100,000 people in the overall population, 70 are in prison. In 2010, Norway opened a new prison which features jogging trails through a forest and small houses where inmates can stay with their families when they visit. Prison guards don't carry guns, and they regularly eat with the prisoners. In this context, the guiding rationale is that prison should try to reflect the world beyond the prison walls (Lee Adams, 'Norway Builds the World's Most Humane Prison', 2010).

These extremely different philosophies illustrate the impact of a culture's specific social, political and legal discourses. However, beyond these differing contexts and philosophies, there are some generalisations that can be drawn out, particularly regarding the inmate population. Most pertinently, it is not representative of the general population. In terms of sex, 90 per cent of prisoners are men. In the USA, the UK and Australia, there are a disproportionate number of people from minority groups: foreigners, asylum seekers and immigrants. Globally, most prisoners have low levels of educational attainment and an erratic employment history. Many have experienced homelessness or the mental healthcare system or have drug dependency issues. In the UK, prisoners are 13 times more likely to have been taken into care by the state as a child, 10 times more likely to have absented themselves from school and 40 times more likely to have three or more mental disorders (Stern, *Creating Criminals*, 2006, p. 32).

This representational disconnect between prison and general populations also encompasses ethnicity and race. A 2010 report, *How Fair Is Britain?*, published by the UK's Equality and Human Rights Commission (EHRC) stated that whereas ethnic minorities account for 11 per cent of the general population in England and Wales, they make up 25 per cent of the prisoner population (p. 172). In the USA, there are more black men in prison than white men, even though black men make up only 12 per cent of the US male population. In 2004, more than 1 in 10 young black men between the ages of 25 and 29 was held within the penal system. The criminalisation and disenfranchisement of the black population is also evidenced in the UK, where black prisoners make up 15 per cent of the prisoner population compared with 2.2 per cent of the general population (p. 172).

This discrepancy between the race, sex, class and social mobility of the prison population and the general population has prompted the allegation that prisons are warehouses for those raised facing societal structural disadvantage. Human rights and penal reform organisations such as Amnesty International, Human Rights Watch and the Howard League for Penal Reform argue that not only are the vast majority of prisoners marginalised within society, but

> evidence shows that the people at the lower end
> of society are least likely to be protected from

crime, the least likely to get redress when crimes
are committed against them, and the most likely
to suffer from injustice within the criminal justice process. (Stern, *Creating Criminals*, p. 73)

This warehousing of the disadvantaged raises many questions about the social cost of the use of imprisonment and
the cyclical impact that this continues to have on society.
Many people who are incarcerated lose their families, their
jobs and their homes. Ninety-five per cent of children of
women in prison are taken into state care or removed from
their family home. The institutionalisation and infantilisa-
tion of prisoners means that it is difficult for them to build
an independent life on release. High rates of recidivism suggest that even with agencies to support rehabilitation and
resettlement, societal attitudes, restricted opportunities
and poverty mean that many ex-prisoners are constructing
a life on quicksand.

The substantial social and economic costs incurred as
a result of these widely acknowledged realities prompt the
question 'What is prison for?' The answer depends on *when*
the question is being asked.

The role of prison within the criminal justice system has
shifted over time. In the twenty-first century it is considered to be a state strategy for crime control, a deterrent
for those contemplating crime and a punitive response for
those who have broken laws. It is also supposed to have a
rehabilitative purpose, preparing inmates to be reintegrated
into life beyond the prison walls – a life where, it is hoped,

they will not re-offend. However, the continued existence and expansion of the prison system since the development of the modern penal system over two centuries ago suggests that it neither controls crime nor rehabilitates. Recidivism statistics in England and Wales indicate that between 60 and 70 per cent of prisoners re-offend within two years of release (Ministry of Justice, 'Reoffending of Adults', 2010). This pattern is evident, to varying degrees, worldwide. If this evidence is taken at face value, prison, as a deterrent to recidivism or as a form of rehabilitation, does not work. Despite this, governments continue to use it as their primary port of punitive call.

Over the past two decades the international prison population has doubled. This is not a reflection of the world becoming a more dangerous place but an outcome of policy. Bluntly, prison is being used more in judicial sentencing. The shift is partly due to a growth in the number of acts which have been identified as criminal, in particular measures related to anti-terrorism, immigration and new technologies. But a greater part is the result of a harsher approach: people are being sent to prison for acts that might previously have warranted a fine or community sentence.

The immediate practical implication is one of space, with politicians demanding that we think about how to accommodate more prisoners rather than interrogate prison's efficacy. Their position is understandable given a tabloid media poised to respond to any reconsideration with headlines that provoke fear and anxiety. In short, the increasing criminalisation of behaviours and the correlative increase in the use of imprisonment have led to unprecedented growth in the number of prisons that are being built globally.

So what does prison cost? In the UK, in 2010, the average cost to the taxpayer of sending someone to prison was £38,000 per year, though this figure varied in different parts of the country. In Northern Ireland, due to the high infrastructural demands and relatively small prison population, the cost per prisoner place was £77,500. In the USA, the cost of prison is estimated at more than $60 billion a year and rising. Incarceration may remove an individual from wider society but the construction of this segregated world isn't cheap. Often it is more costly for the state to sentence someone for a year, to a place where there are few educative or developmental opportunities, than it is to invest in them through formal education and the possibilities it may offer on release. This paradox leaves the state open to the accusation that it is invested in neoliberal capitalist models which supposedly support punishment and rehabilitation, while in effect maintaining societal structural disadvantage, class distinctions and social immobility.

To accommodate the growth in the global prison population, some governments, particularly those of the USA and the UK, are turning to private companies to build and manage these new institutions, fuelling a highly profitable corrections industry and reframing the economy of punishment. This raises a number of urgent ethical questions. Private companies are in the business of making money. If the prison population continues to rise, the opportunity for business expansion and profit thrives. The publicly articulated political desire to reduce the number of people being imprisoned runs counter to the financial interests of shareholders of companies running private prisons. The UK's Prison Reform Trust argues that private prisons are, in effect, human exploitation:

> A prison sentence is the most severe form of punishment in this country and it should be the duty of the state to administer the deprivation of liberty. Without proper public and parliamentary debate, questions of whether it is ethical for private companies to make financial gains from imprisonment are in danger of being swept aside through expedience and in the name of modernization. (*Private Punishment: Who Profits?* 2005, p. 15)

In England, laws pertaining to commercial confidentiality prevent government from revealing financial or operational details, making it more difficult for Parliament and the electorate to hold these companies publicly accountable. But what is clear from what *is* publicly available – the companies' annual reports and the profits outlined within them – is that prisons are big business. G4S (Group 4 Securicor) has over 600,000 employees in 110 countries; its pre-tax profits for the first nine months of 2010 were £143 million. Corrections Corporation of America's facilities have capacity for over 80,000 prisoners across the USA and, despite the worldwide recession, the company posted an increase in profits in 2009.

These figures illustrate the representational gap between the images of incarceration that populate the cultural imagination and the reality of a multi-billion-pound economy of punishment, subject to neoliberal market forces, which does little to deter crime or rehabilitate those who have been convicted. This gap fosters public misinformation, fear and a lack of critical engagement with the role of prison in society. It allows the corrections industry to thrive, with little critical discourse about the morality of the business of punishment. How a state chooses to punish and the value given to the criminal body reveal much about the ideals of that society. If we fail to consider how a society responds to those who infringe its laws we abdicate responsibility for them.

How theatre and performance help us understand prison

The theatre practices considered in this book traverse the physical and imagined boundaries between life inside and outside prison in order to engage with incarceration as a cultural metaphor and a material technology of state power and control. At the same time, the book is careful not to mythologise the prisoner as 'victim' and recognises the complex social, cultural and economic contexts which frame the use of imprisonment.

There are three areas of investigation in *Theatre & Prison*. First, I consider the shifting role of prison, informed by ideas of representation, narrative and audience, in the performance of punishment and justice. Second, I examine specific dramatic texts and productions which have provoked public understanding, debate and action in relation to the ideology and practice of prison. Some critical attention has been paid to prison drama in terms of narrative and character, but little to how it interrogates the context and ideology of its setting. Finally, I address theatre in prison. Since the mid-1980s, there has been a growing field of theatre practice and scholarship in this area which is variously referred to as 'prison theatre', 'theatre in prison' or 'applied theatre'. Much of the documentation of, and therefore access to, theatre practice in prison is based on work by US or UK artists and academics. There have been invaluable contributions from Michael Balfour, Paul Heritage, Jenny Hughes and James Thompson revealing the negotiated complexity of working in this context. However, there has been no survey of the practices of theatre in prison which draws the methodological politics of these practices across the twentieth and twenty-first centuries into conversation with each other. *Theatre & Prison* begins to address this gap, acknowledging that although each prison institution is distinct, operating in a specific cultural and historical context, some commonalities and generalisations can be drawn across different models of penal practice.

The idea of prison is so embedded in our juridical, architectural and cultural landscapes that it is easy to assume it has been, and will continue to be, a permanent feature of society. The sociologist David Garland argues that the lack of questioning about prison as punishment is 'a consequence of the obscuring and reassuring effect of established institutions, rather than the transparent rationality of penal practices themselves' (*Punishment and Modern Society*, p. 3). Throughout this book I argue that theatre and performance practice can make visible the institution of prison, allowing us to critically examine its social, economic and cultural impact.

Part One

the performance of punishment

Before I address theatre practice *in* prison and theatre practice which engages *with* imprisonment I will consider the role of prison in the dramaturgy of crime, punishment and justice.

Since ancient times, societies have developed systems of justice designed to protect that which is valuable – life, liberty, property and reputation – and to administer punishments to those who commit, in the words of the criminologist Nils Christie, 'unwanted acts' which threaten these values (*A Suitable Amount of Crime*, 2004, p. 24). Punishment is, potentially, about many things. For society, it is about crime control, public security and the restoration of social relationships. For the individual who has committed a crime, punishment may be regarded as retribution, or as an opportunity for reformation and rehabilitation. It is an integral part of the narrative of justice: a crime is committed, a criminal is apprehended, a fair trial is held, a sentence is declared, a punishment is administered and justice is seen to be done – a progressive, linear storyline where everything appears to work out in the end. The public audience for this performance of justice produced by the state are citizens, subjects and, increasingly since World War II, international independent watchdogs and human rights organisations.

Although the idea of justice as a set of fair, equitable and transparent 'arrangements of relationships in a society' was developed by the ancient Greeks, the question of how punishment might support the administration of justice has led to an elastic and responsive set of ideas and practices (A. C. Grayling, *Ideas That Matter*, 2009, p. 201). Garland's investigation of the sociology of punishment reveals it to be 'a complex set of interrelated processes and institutions, rather than a uniform object or event' (*Punishment and Modern Society*, p. 6). Crime and punishment are not stable entities. *What* a society chooses to punish and *how* it chooses to do so depend on the specific social, political and economic concerns which shape that society. Christie proposes that the word 'crime' is 'like a sponge. The term can loosely absorb lots of acts – and people – when external circumstances make that useful' (*A Suitable Amount of Crime*, pp. ix–x). For example, murder, rape, robbery, embezzlement and arson are recognised as unwanted, criminal acts in every country (Stern, *Creating Criminals*, p. 6). However, other behaviours, such as abortion, drug taking and association with non-familial members of the opposite sex, are accepted in some societies but deemed unwanted, illegal and punishable by law in others. New laws are continually made that reflect the interests and concerns of a globalised world. A recent review of the UK Labour Party's term of office from 1997 to 2010 revealed that it made over 4,300 new laws during that period (Dowling, '4,300: How Labour Has Created a New Crime Every Day since 1997', 2010). Some of these laws appear to be useful and necessary – particularly those responding to developments in technology and the traffic in personal data – but others appear to be farcical in their extremity. At the time of writing, in the UK it is illegal to 'disturb a pack of eggs when instructed not to do so by an officer' or to fail to use the correct weighing system for herring and mackerel. These examples illustrate the fluidity and expansiveness of the term 'crime' and evidence the increasing reach of state surveillance and intervention. As a consequence, as more human acts are considered to be criminal, there are greater opportunities for law enforcement to intervene, leading to a subsequent rise in administration of punishment including penal sentences.

Punishment

So how do states respond to crime and administer punishment? Each state has a penal system which 'is an embodiment of its power to control by threats, force, suppression and even destruction … whatever threatens and inconveniences it, or disrupts its efficiencies' (Grayling, *Ideas That Matter*, p. 295). But, like the concept of crime, practices of punishment are historically and socially variable, reflecting the values of the society that performs them. In the early twenty-first century, in most societies, these practices have manifested as fines, restrictions, community sentences and imprisonment, impacting as they do on money, time, liberty and reputation. While it is universally agreed that death is the highest tariff that a state can impose, there is also divergence: many countries reject the death penalty, while others, such as the USA, China and Afghanistan, retain the right to call upon it as the ultimate sanction.

For the most part, this range of measures is presented as being reactive, a response to transgression. But punishments also act pre-emptively, as warnings and deterrents to those who have not *yet* committed a crime: these publicly articulated demonstrations of power illustrate the state's response to acts which threaten its stability. Today, when the state is most at risk – in cases of terrorism, murder, rape, theft and fraud – the measure it most commonly responds with is prison, a form of punishment that we now take for granted as being both punitive and rehabilitative. There is a sense that we have inherited a stable idea, that 'we've always had prisons' and that their role within the narrative of punishment and justice has always behaved in a recognisable way. A brief glance at the historical context reveals that this is not the case.

A brief history of prison

This section draws primarily on English penal practice, which has informed the ideology and architecture of prisons in many other countries. Historically, prisons have had three uses: custodial, coercive and punitive (Rod Morgan and Alison Liebling, 'Imprisonment: An Expanding Scene',

2007, p. 1105). Until the end of the eighteenth century, prisons were places of containment rather than punishment. Criminal bodies convicted of crimes were held within them until such time as the state called them forward to administer corporeal or capital punishment. Prisons were an eclectic range of physical spaces – dungeons, rooms attached to courthouses, cottages and mansions serving a practical rather than ideological function. Like workhouses, orphanages and houses of correction, prisons were private enterprises run for profit rather than part of a government-led juridical system. The bodies within them had an economic value which reflected market concerns. Prisoners had to pay for their food and board, and there was a system of accommodation that reflected the means of the prisoners: those with little possibility of paying their debts could find themselves in windowless dungeons with rats, disease-ridden inmates and the dead; well-to-do prisoners, on the other hand, could buy the privilege of a bar, decent lodgings and freedom to leave the prison during the day. Unlike today, prisons in England in the seventeenth century were accessible to the public: tradesmen, families and curiosity seekers were part of the daily ebb and flow of prison life. Debtors' prisons frequently had communities of families born and raised within the prison walls while waiting for a parent's debts to be paid off. The conditions within prisons were appalling: disease, corruption, extortion and brutality were given licence by tyrannical jailers who profited from the accumulation of misfortune on their watch. Today such behaviour would be condemned as cruel and unusual punishment, something additional to the deprivation of liberty. However, in the eighteenth century it was unremarkable, as the 'real' punishment was enacted upon criminal bodies, beyond the prison walls, as part of a public spectacle.

The spectacle of punishment

Flogging, branding, stoning, mutilation and whipping were common corporeal and public punishments in western societies until the end of the eighteenth century. Death – immediate or prolonged – was induced by hanging, garrotting, burying alive, burning or decapitation. Penal servitude and transportation to penal colonies demanded that criminal bodies continued to be publicly defined in terms of their deviance. This panoply of corporeal and capital punishments 'reflected a particular attitude toward the body, an attitude that ... gave little thought to pain or bodily integrity' (Pieter Spierenburg, 'The Body and the State: Early Modern Europe', 1997, p. 45). Public torture and execution were choreographed events with staged conventions and a dramaturgical structure adhered to by the state which produced the spectacle, and understood by the public audience who witnessed it.

This relationship between the state and the pubic was particularly evident in eighteenth-century hanging days. These sprawling, carnivalesque events attracted thousands of people to witness the final journey of the condemned criminal body from this world to the next. In London, at this time, the convict processed in an open cart from Newgate prison along the two-mile stretch to the gallows at Tyburn (now Marble Arch). Church bells announced the event, street vendors hawked their wares and crowds thronged the streets, jostling for the best view of the scaffold (Spierenburg, 'Body and State'; Peter Linebaugh, *The London Hanged: Crime and Civil Society in the Eighteenth Century*, 2003). 'Lethal Theatre: Performance, Punishment and the Death Penalty', Dwight Conquergood's 2002 analysis of the death penalty in the USA over a period of more than 300 years, illustrates the magnetic draw of the *event* of the execution for a general public. Referring to hangings in Puritan New England, he details examples of people travelling over 50 miles and gathering for a week before the 'tragical spectacle' and argues, 'In terms of sheer audience size, executions were the most popular performance genre in seventeenth- and eighteenth-century America' (p. 344). Corporeal and capital punishment was a public event which demonstrated the absolute power of the state upon the individual body of an errant subject or citizen.

The language of theatricality, spectacle and entertainment is often used by historians recounting these events. Spierenburg illustrates this when he states,

> Theatrical punishment and the scaffold were closely linked in early modern Europe. Noncapital physical punishments, though not everywhere carried out on a scaffold-like structure, were usually dispensed in public, giving them a theatrical character. The legal infliction of pain and

death was a show before an audience. ('Body and State', p. 47)

The scaffold set the stage for a drama of justice with stock characters, a prescribed narrative and a climactic ending. The criminal, the executioner and the religious official all had their parts to play. Their clothing and props re-inscribed their roles: white brocade in the condemned's hat was a symbol of victory or innocence, the hood of the executioner masked the individual who killed on behalf of the state and the Bible was a reminder that all acts were carried out in front of an omniscient God. The theatricality of the performance of punishment, particularly the staging of the criminal body and the semiotics of the event to be read by the audience, is playfully exploited in Caryl Churchill's *Softcops* (Barbican, London, 1984), an animated staging of aspects of Michel Foucault's *Discipline and Punish* (1977). Set in France at the end of the eighteenth century, the play opens with Pierre, who produces public punishment events on behalf of the state:

> *A high scaffold is being erected. PIERRE is anxiously supervising and helping drape it in black cloth and put up posters and placards. A crocodile of young BOYS in uniform crosses the stage with their HEADMASTER, circles and stops in front of the scaffold.*
>
> ...
>
> PIERRE. ... Where are the red ribbons? Look children, red is a symbol of blood and passion,

the blood shed by passion and the blood shed
by Reason in justice and grief. Grief is sym-
bolised of course by black. ... The procession comes down the hill so the crowd can
watch its approach. Doleful music specially
composed. I've written a speech for the magistrate and one for each of the condemned
men. ...

The procession comes in: the MAGISTRATE in black;
the EXECUTIONER in red; the MUSICIANS and
GUARDS in black and red; black-draped cart; the
PRISONER in the cart in black except for his right
hand in a red glove which he holds up. A placard
round his neck: Jacques Duval, thief.

(pp. 5–7)

This scene explicitly addresses the performative nature of
punishment. Within this dramaturgical structure, the condemned gave their final, scripted speeches – some repented;
some proclaimed their innocence; some boldly celebrated
their crimes. *This* moment, rather than the instant when
the mortal body was extinguished, was the critical climax
of the event. In a Christian society, the fate of the immortal
soul of the condemned was unknown. If they were genu-
inely repentant they would be granted forgiveness by God
and their soul would be given access to Heaven. If they were
false in their iterations or blasphemed, their soul would be
condemned to Hell. State justice could be felt by the convict
only in this life; the final act in this narrative of justice was

performed by God in the afterlife. The structure and staging manipulated audiences to identify with the condemned and, according to Conquergood,

> encouraged a deeply sympathetic, theatrical iden-
> tification in which the spectators could imagi-
> natively exchange places with the condemned,
> instead of holding themselves aloof in distanced
> judgement. The ideal spectator at execution
> became a deeply engaged performative witness.
> ('Lethal Theatre', p. 351)

This awareness of the 'show' of the execution and the implication of the audience as an integral part of it is further illustrated by Spierenburg's account of death by burning in France, a practice common until the eighteenth century ('Body and State', p. 49). A convict, about to suffer a prolonged and excruciating death, could earn a *retentum* – death by strangulation prior to immolation – by naming accomplices in his crime. This had to be done secretly so that 'the audience would not notice that the show was a fake; authorities did not want the mercy shown to an individual offender to cause the public to doubt the severity of justice' (p. 49).

These spectacular state interventions upon the body of the criminal served two crucial functions in the maintenance of order: they warned the public of the outcomes of criminal acts and, as performances of justice, made an abstract idea visible and corporeally significant. However, by the end of the eighteenth century, these public narratives of punishment and justice had been rewritten. Executions were carried out in private, behind closed doors, and the prison went from being a place where people waited to be punished to being a site of punishment and reformation.

Private justice: the emergence of the penitentiary

There were two reasons for this. Enlightenment thinking emerging in the eighteenth century informed attitudes about the sanctity and dignity of human life and the relationship between the state and the individual. Concurrent with this was the shift in power and leadership from the aristocracy to 'the merchants, factory owners, the managers of resources and labour', whose business needed 'an orderly work force' (Bender, *Imagining the Penitentiary*, 1987, pp. 30–31). In this context, the value of the criminal body was revised. Capital punishment and transportation removed bodies from a potential workforce. Reformed convicts, with life and limbs intact, could perform productively in it.

So what was the idea and practice of the new prison? Penal historians, philosophers and sociologists, including George Rusche and Otto Kirchheimer, Michel Foucault, Michael Ignatieff and David Garland (see further reading at the end of this book), have illustrated how the politics of punishment is subject to market forces. At times when there was a shortage of workers, these criminal non-productive bodies were held in houses of correction and hired as cheap labour. At times of high unemployment these bodies offered little economic potential in a domestic market and, for punishment, were transported to colonies where their penal labour had a value in the manufacturing of a new world.

The American War of Independence put an end to Britain's export of convict bodies across the Atlantic. An alternative had to be found. Convicts could be released, sent to new lands such as Australia, destroyed, or contained and put to non-productive work such as the everlasting staircase, a mechanical device prescient of the contemporary gym's step machine. Political and economic contexts converged: an expanding population being held captive in prisons, Enlightenment thinking about the relationship between the individual and the state, a growing rationalist approach towards law and justice, and the pioneering work of John Howard, whose *The State of the Prisons* (1777) surveyed and condemned the material and moral state of prisons. This critical mass gave birth to the idea of a nationalised prison system which served as punishment *and* reformation.

The idea and design of prison as reformative, pioneered in England in the late eighteenth century, has, due to the country's colonial reach, informed the development of prisons in many countries. The administrative and architectural infrastructure of this eighteenth-century system is inscribed in contemporary penal practice around the globe.

Prisons were to be renamed 'penitentiaries', echoing Christian ideas of sin, penitence, forgiveness and redemption. These new institutions were founded on the criminological theory of voluntarism, proposed by John Locke and Cesare Beccaria, that individuals have free will and that a criminal *chooses* to carry out an illegal act. Therefore, if a criminal was held in separate and silent confinement he would reflect on his crimes, see the error of his ways, reform, and return to society and *choose* not to commit crime.

With the advent of the penitentiary, the narrative of justice was dramaturgically restructured: the convict was no longer arrested, condemned, punished and judged in the afterlife. Instead, he was arrested, sentenced to imprisonment, reformed and released. The convict's fate after punishment no longer unfolded in Heaven or Hell at the discretion of an omnipotent God; rather it was lived on Earth, where the reformed prisoner had the opportunity to model a penitent, good and productive life. This new narrative of justice was formalised in law in the 1779 Penitentiary Act and materialised through a national prison-building campaign that saw the construction of specially designed institutions which acted upon the body, mind and soul of the offender. Unlike the public displays of corporeal and capital punishment, the penitentiary was a technology of state power which invisibly guided the criminal body towards reform through the manipulation of time, space and action. Prisons were no longer just a thing – a place, a building to contain bodies – but a narrative idea which was articulated through architecture where '[t]he doctrine of reform' was written into 'the practicalities of construction' (Robin Evans, *The Fabrication of Virtue*, 1982, p. 115).

Within this new formulation, the position and role of the audience for the performance of punishment changed.

The retributive hand of the state and the offending body that it had once marked, ripped and destroyed were both withdrawn from public view. The prison walls now not only kept convicts in, but kept the public out. While the interior space performed upon the deviant subjects, the exterior architecture also played a role in shaping public perception of the idea of prison. Imposing Gothic frontages articulated the secure, opaque physical separation of one world from the other while hinting at the harsh, horrific, hidden world they enclosed. Denied access to, or participation in, this new process of punishment and justice, the public was left to let its imagination run wild with hellish possibilities.

The newly established audiences for prison *as* punishment were the prisoners themselves and the eye of the state. Ideas of viewing – particularly monitoring, self-observation and constant visibility – informed the construction of the new prisons which sought to reconstruct the character of the criminal. This system positioned the criminal body as a performer expected to play his role as the penitent convict. His movements were choreographed in a 24-hour cycle of precisely monitored, disciplining and reforming activity which was repeated throughout the duration of his sentence. In this context, the prisoner's uniform – the broad-arrowed uniform, the striped garments and the prison cap with its long peak that was pulled down to mask the prisoner's face – became a costume which contributed to the reiteration of this identity and, through its shape, texture and pattern, contributed to the punishment of the offender (Juliet Ash,

Dress Behind Bars, 2010). On release, the inmate's embodied habit of reform would ensure that he performed as a good and productive citizen.

This rebuilding of character through the manipulation of the body in space was supported through the internal architecture of prison. The radial designs of William Blackburn featured in many of the early English prisons and included a central viewing point around which were constructed tiers of cells which were equally visible. This design allowed an economy of surveillance in which a single guard could monitor both a vast area and a large number of convicts. Jeremy Bentham further developed this concept in his panopticon. The term 'panopticon' is often used loosely to refer to any prison built on a radial design. However, it is important to specify the panopticon as both an idea and an architectural articulation which facilitates the possibility of an omnipresent authoritative gaze that not only monitors behaviour but creates an environment of self-observation among the criminals, who modify their behaviour accordingly. Bentham's design was highly theatrical: individual cells had doors made porous with gratings and were backlit so that the inmate could be seen at all times. These 'small theatres, in which each actor is alone, perfectly individualised and constantly visible', offered neither physical nor emotional sanctuary (Foucault, *Discipline and Punish*, p. 200). Once again, Churchill illustrates this concept dramatically in *Softcops* when Pierre, the producer of public executions we met earlier, is in conversation with Bentham. Bentham invites Pierre to play the role of the prisoner by sitting alone on the stage, while he plays the role of the guard and disappears behind the central watch tower, a curtain, to watch him. Pierre sits. Time passes, and Pierre gets increasingly agitated and anxious:

> PIERRE. Mr Bentham?
> Am I doing it properly?
> Do you want me to draw some conclusions? It's not comfortable being watched when you can't see the person watching you. You can see all of us prisoners and we can't see each other. We can't communicate by tapping on the walls because you are watching us. Is that right? Mr Bentham? I understand how it works. Can I get up now?
>
> *BENTHAM comes out of the back of the stand unseen by PIERRE. He creeps round so that he's behind him while he talks. BENTHAM giggles silently.*
>
> …I think it's most ingenious, Mr Bentham, an excellent means of control. Without chains, without pain. Can I get up now?
>
> (pp. 39–40)

This brief scene illustrates the principle of the panopticon in action: the idea rather than the presence of the viewer affects the behaviour of the person who thinks he is being watched. In his original plan, Bentham had wanted to take this idea even further by making the exterior prison wall glass so that the public could witness the convicts and the convicts could see themselves reflected in society's eyes. Although the panopticon was never fully realised during Bentham's lifetime, adaptations of it were built in Illinois, USA, and the Netherlands. The idea of the panopticon carries an enduring symbolic weight of the power of state surveillance to mould docile, productive bodies in an industrialised and post-industrialised world. The legacy of this is evidenced in contemporary debates about Big Brother society, closed-circuit television and identity cards.

Disrupted narratives of reformation

After a wave of extensive prison building during the nineteenth century, growing rates of imprisonment and recidivism undermined the idea of prison as threat, punishment or reformation of character. There was a crisis in the narrative of rational punishment. The idea of the penitentiary, made real through the construction of a nationalised prison system, failed to dissuade people from carrying out criminal acts or to transform the behaviour of those already convicted of such acts.

Assumptions about crime and punishment had to be reconsidered. However, the physical remnants of previous philosophical and political thinking made this a difficult task. In the following centuries, new directions in justice, crime, punishment and social control always had to contend with the material existence of a mode of punishment that had been very heavily invested in, politically and economically: the infrastructure of the eighteenth- and nineteenth-century prison system still informs the experience of those who live and work within the system today.

In 1993, the announcement by the Conservative Home Secretary, Michael Howard, that 'prisons work' reaffirmed the UK's commitment to the use of imprisonment and catalysed the expansion of the prison system. At the beginning of the twenty-first century, the rapid expansion and privatisation of the prison service illustrate the impact of globalisation on contemporary penal practice and the representation and value of the criminal body within it. In this context, a criminal body is considered to be a non-productive social body which, prior to conviction, is likely to have been unemployed, dependent on welfare and a drain on a capitalist economy which values work and the ability to earn and spend money. However, in a neoliberal capitalist economy of punishment which advocates the privatisation of the corrections industry, these lives suddenly become valuable: a rise in rates of incarceration demands a rise in the number of prisons being built, providing employment for the people who manage them and business opportunities for the support services which supply them. The privatisation of the prison industry is making these non-productive bodies perform, albeit without agency, in the capitalist global economy. Their non-productivity, their non-performance as law-abiding citizens, makes them a valuable commodity in the multi-billion-pound global corrections industry.

Questioning the idea of prison in the twenty-first century uncovers a network of power relations between the individual and the state, revealing the economic concerns which re-inscribe a status quo of hierarchy and control. Thinking about the shifting role of the prison in the performance of punishment helps us think about the staging of the criminal body, the role of narrative in the demonstration of justice and the position of the audience in the public and private administrations of punishment. We are positioned by the state as the audience for justice. Without a critical reflection on our own position as such, we risk being passive observers, assuming that long-standing mechanisms of state control are just and 'natural' – that they are the ways things have always been and will always be.

Part Two

theatre about prison

Since the end of the eighteenth century, prisons have been designed to keep convicts in and the public, and its gaze, out. Their opaque inner workings are made partly visible through cultural representations eager to exploit the setting's rich possibilities for dramatic action.

In addition to an extensive array of prison literature and film, there are many plays in which some or all of the action takes place behind prison walls: John Gay's *The Beggars' Opera* (Lincoln's Inn Fields Theatre, London, 1728), Brendan Behan's *The Quare Fella* (Pike Theatre, Dublin, 1954), Miguel Piñero's *Short Eyes* (Riverside Church, New York, 1974), Rona Munro's *Iron* (Traverse Theatre, Edinburgh, 2002) and Rebecca Lenkiewicz's *Her Naked Skin* (National Theatre, London, 2008) provide a small sample.

Theatre has also given us the sub-genre of the prison musical, usually based on a successful television series, play or novel. Examples include *Bad Girls: The Musical* (West

Yorkshire Playhouse, Leeds, 2006), *Prisoner Cell Block H: The Musical* (Queen's Theatre, London, 1995), *Chicago* (46th Street Theatre, New York, 1975) and *Kiss of the Spider Woman* (Shaftesbury Theatre, London, 1992). *Dead Man Walking* has been made into an opera (War Memorial Opera House, San Francisco, 2000), and *The Shawshank Redemption* (Gaiety Theatre, Dublin, 2009) and *Porridge* (Gordon Craig Theatre, Stevenage, 2009) have recently been produced in large-scale commercial venues in Ireland and the UK, respectively.

Elsewhere, context and location fuse in site-specific productions. Teatro Vertigem's *Apocalipse 1,11* (2000) opened in São Paulo's notorious Carandiru penitentiary, and Tinderbox's *Convictions* (2000) was staged in the Crumlin Road courthouse and jail in Belfast. Both venues were recently decommissioned buildings of state punishment and justice, and the productions engaged directly with the penal, social and political histories of these sites.

All these plays and productions staged (sometimes literally) in prisons reaffirm our cultural rather than our experiential familiarity with penal institutions. Even the site-specific productions allow us only partial access to the worlds within the decommissioned buildings. David Wilson and Sean O'Sullivan, in their book *Images of Incarceration: Representations of Prison in Film and Television Drama* (2004), argue that

> [d]rama provides people with the imaginative resources which help them visualise, or imagine

the nature of the world. It can be suggested that people are much more receptive to arguments about things outside their own experience if they possess a cultural model or metaphor which helps them visualise it. (p. 14)

The core argument here is that cultural representations and narratives of prison, particularly on television and in film, help us to understand it. But do they, particularly as the nature of the depiction is inherently unstable? The original cinema poster for the exploitation film *The Big Doll House* (1971) announces the following about the movie's female inmates: 'Their bodies were caged but not their desires. They would do anything for a man – or to him.' This offers a very different 'imaginative resource' from the social drama presented in *The Weak and the Wicked* (1954), which follows the lives of a number of women during and after their experience of prison. Elsewhere, the fictional world of HMP Slade in the BBC sit-com *Porridge* (1974–78) imagines a cultural model which bears little or no resemblance to the one presented in the American television series *Oz* (1997–2003).

Not all representations of prison and prisoners do the same cultural work. Some reiterate imaginatively limited narrative tropes and stereotypes while others prompt insight and new understandings. Some invite affective responses of shock or titillation while others provoke effective response and political action. Within theatre and performance there are many examples of theatre makers who attempt the latter, using form and content to critically engage with the politics of imprisonment. Miguel Piñero's *Short Eyes*, written while he was a prisoner at Ossining Correctional Facility, details the politics of race and the culture of violence condoned within prison walls. Institutional racism in the English prison system has been tackled by Tanika Gupta in *Gladiator Games* (Crucible, Sheffield, 2005), and, since 1979, Clean Break theatre company have used theatre to campaign for a greater understanding of the issues that affect women within the criminal justice system.

In the following sections I examine three dramatic texts and productions which have reframed representations of prison within the imaginative landscape: John Galsworthy's *Justice* (Duke of York's Theatre, London, and Glasgow Repertory Theatre, 1910), Tennessee Williams' *Not About Nightingales* (National Theatre, London, 1998) and John Herbert's *Fortune and Men's Eyes* (Actors' Playhouse, New York, 1967). These writers use theatre to report from within the prison, exposing and condemning abuse within it and revealing the hegemonic power relations which shape it. These dramatic texts are products of their time, responses to specific events and urgent appeals to the public to pay attention to the state's performance of punishment and justice which is carried out on their behalf.

Justice

John Galsworthy was an English novelist, playwright and activist whose campaign for penal reform, early in the twentieth century, culminated in his play *Justice*, staged simultaneously at the Duke of York's Theatre in London and Glasgow Repertory Theatre in 1910.

There was, at this time, an acknowledgement in political circles that something needed to be done about 'the prison problem'. As discussed earlier, the idea of the English national prison service was realised through an extensive, costly building programme. By the early twentieth century, this 'new' prison system had been in operation for nearly 100 years, and although it had become clear that the penitentiary as a site for character transformation was a narrative idea that didn't work in practice, the development of the architectural and administrative infrastructure meant that it was, just as it is today, politically difficult to imagine or enact an alternative.

Justice is a four-act play reflecting, in tone and style, the 'new dramatist' movement pioneered by G. B. Shaw and Gerhart Hauptmann, who sought to use the theatre as a means to discuss pressing social issues. The play tells the story of John Falder, a young legal clerk in love with Ruth Honeywell, a woman married to a violent drunk. When she appears at Falder's home, her clothing ripped and with bruising on her neck, Falder fears for her life. Later that day, deranged with worry, he forges a company cheque to fund Ruth and her children's escape. The forgery is discovered and the wheels of justice begin to turn. As the play unfolds, it reflects the assumed linear narrative of justice: a wrong is done, the perpetrator is found, the law is upheld and punishment is dispensed. Falder is arrested, tried and sentenced to three years' penal servitude.

In the early twentieth century, convicted prisoners in the UK began their sentences with a period of solitary confinement that lasted from three to nine months. This was a legacy of the 'separate and silent' system that characterised the early nationalised prison regime, which held that a period of isolation would induce reflection, penance and reformation of the prisoner's soul. As a star-class prisoner – an adult first-time offender – the fictional Falder would serve three months in solitary confinement with his conscience and the Bible for company.

Over the past century, due to extensive debate about solitary confinement as torture and psychological studies which have evidenced its detrimental impact on mental health and well-being, its use has been radically reduced. In most contemporary prison contexts, when solitary confinement is employed it is an unusual and brief disciplinary act. The American Supermax prisons are anomalous in their standard continuous use of it. As ideas about the rationale of prisons shifted in early twentieth-century penal thinking, from punishment and reformation to rehabilitation, the nature of solitary confinement was also questioned. Act Three, Scene Three of *Justice* presents Falder alone in his cell. Galsworthy's research, visiting prisons and interviewing inmates, is illustrated in the detailed description of the set:

> Falder's cell, a whitewashed space thirteen feet broad by seven deep, and nine feet high, with a rounded ceiling. The floor is shiny blackened bricks. The barred window, with a ventilator, is

high up in the middle of the end wall. In the middle of the opposite end wall is the narrow door,
in a corner are the mattress and bedding rolled
up (two blankets, two sheets, and a coverlet).
Above them is a quarter-circular wooden shelf,
on which is a Bible and several little devotional
books, piled in a symmetrical pyramid...In
another corner is the wooden frame of a bed,
standing on end. (p. 426)

At a time before whistle-blowing television documentaries,
Galsworthy was using theatre as a medium to publicly docu-
ment realities of prison life that would have been far removed
from the experience or imagination of his audience.

The scene in Falder's cell has no spoken text, only a
description of his actions:

Falder, in his stockings, is seen standing motionless, with his head inclined towards the door, lis-
tening. He moves a little closer to the door ... He
is trying harder and harder to hear something,
any little thing that is going on outside. He
springs suddenly upright – as if at a sound – and
remains perfectly motionless...Then, turning
abruptly, he begins pacing the cell, moving his
head, like an animal pacing its cage. (p. 426)

Throughout the scene, Galsworthy reveals how the abstract
idea of justice and punishment becomes the sensate torment

of an individual. The audience witness Falder unravel in his solitary confinement, the very same environment that the prison administration advocate for the reformation of character. Solitary confinement might impact character, but not necessarily in the constructive ways that the founders of the penitentiary imagined.

When Falder is released, he is a broken man, unable to get a firm foothold in a world that now judges him as a criminal rather than a citizen. No company will employ him. In desperation, his lover, Honeywell, approaches Falder's old employers and begs them to give him a job. Just as it looks like Falder will be given another chance, a police officer appears to arrest him for failing to report his whereabouts to the police and for forging references in an attempt to secure work. Unable to imagine a return to prison, Falder leaps from the window and kills himself.

The play presents audiences with a narrative full of emotional hooks: an illicit love affair, a criminal act committed in a moment of passionate despair, a public and dramatic arrest, a courtroom trial and a tragic suicide. It would be easy to imagine that an Edwardian audience could exit the theatre feeling exhilarated by the emotional whirlwind of the evening and leave the concerns of the play in the West End. However, the production activated something in the public conscience. It provoked a debate which spilled beyond the Duke of York's Theatre into 'tear-stained letters' from members of the public to the then Home Secretary, Winston Churchill, begging him to reconsider the use of solitary confinement. Churchill, who had seen the play, entered into discussion with Galsworthy, who urged reforms, including home leave, more exercise and the abolition of solitary confinement, arguing that '[r]evenge, which may be a justifiable individual emotion, is not a justifiable official or State emotion' (quoted in James Gindin, *John Galsworthy's Life and Art*, 1987, p. 206).

Since the 1895 Gladstone Report on penal policy there had been some discussion but little action nationally to address both prison's function and the material conditions experienced by inmates. Galsworthy's play hit an already exposed nerve. By the end of summer 1910, the government had passed legislation improving the treatment of prisoners which included the reduction of solitary confinement from three months to one month. Churchill acknowledged Galsworthy's, and therefore the public's, contribution to the reforms when he said, '[T]here can be no question that your admirable play bore a most important part in creating that atmosphere of sympathy and interest which is so noticeable upon the subject at this present time' (*Galsworthy's Life and Art*, p. 207).

Justice was a bold statement which revealed how the machinery of justice that seeks to protect society can also crush it. In the play, Galsworthy argued that solitary confinement was cruel, retributive and additional to the punishment of the removal of liberty. But *Justice* is not only a play about solitary confinement and reform of specific penal practices. It problematises moral simplicity by presenting Falder as a man who tries to right a wrong (the abuse of his lover and her children by her husband) and in so doing commits a criminal act. Yet, for Falder, not to respond to the imminent danger facing Ruth Honeywell was morally incomprehensible. *Justice* is an invitation to the public to question their assumptions about the relationship between crime and punishment and to consider its actuality rather than its abstraction. It is also an appeal for the public to recognise their own hypocrisy. If prisons are being presented to the public as sites of reform and rehabilitation for the criminal, then the society into which criminals return should acknowledge this rather than extending the sentence of shame and exclusion beyond the duration of the prison term.

Galsworthy's play – staged in London and Glasgow in 1910 and in Boston and New York in 1916 – added to a political momentum on both continents at that time, contributing to a tipping-point moment in penal reform. It revealed the capacity of theatre not only to affect its audience but to provoke public understanding and political action.

Not About Nightingales

Where Galsworthy examined punishment meted out by the state, other dramatists have directly addressed unofficial acts of torture and abuse within the prison system. Alexander Paterson, the radical reform-minded Prison Commissioner of England and Wales from 1922 to 1946, stated, 'Men are sent to prison as punishment, not *for* punishment' (S. K. Ruck, *Paterson on Prisons*, 1951, p. 13). His comment belies an underlying truth that although, in principle, the punishment of being sent to prison is the deprivation of liberty, the reality (and perhaps the hope of those wanting criminals to be made pay for their acts against society) is that bad things happen in prison – acts of brutality, torture or indignity. These are additional punishments to that which someone has been sentenced to: acts with which the state may be complicit through choice or neglect.

Not About Nightingales, an early play by Tennessee Williams written in 1938 and forgotten for nearly 60 years, was premiered at the National Theatre, London, in 1998. Although Williams places the action in 'a large American prison' and states that '[t]he conditions which the play presents are those of no particular prison but a composite picture of many' (p. 1), the play is clearly a direct response to the Klondike massacre in Philadelphia County Prison, USA, in 1938. The 22 episodic scenes, introduced with captions and by an announcer, are heavily influenced by the Living Newspaper of the 1930s Federal Theatre Project, where the documentary style reiterates the 'real-life' content of the play.

The Klondike massacre began with inmates complaining about the quality and monotony of the food they received and the subsequent impact of this on their health. The prison authorities refused to address their concerns and the inmates went on hunger strike. The institutional response was to punish the men for their insubordination rather than to take their concerns seriously. Twenty-five men were sent to the Klondike, a sealed building with banks of radiators which created a furnace-like atmosphere. Inside this 'little suburb of hell' (p. 41), the men's respiratory and circulatory systems were stretched to collapse as they attempted to cool their bodies in the boiling heat. Scalding and asphyxiation were inevitable as the men were cooked alive. Four men died and 21 suffered critical injuries. The horrific brutality of this act and the failure of the subsequent trial to convict many of the prison staff for the atrocity caused a public furore.

In *Nightingales*, Williams demands that audiences not be complacent in their position of moral outrage. He frames the beginning and end of the play with an identical scene which acts as a critical proposition to the audience. In it, we hear the sound of day-trippers on a pleasure boat which sails past the prison twice a day and the voice of the boat-guide saying,

> This is the Lorelei excursion steamer, all-day trip ... Sight-seeing, dancing, entertainment with Lorelei Lou and her eight Lorelights! ... Sun's bright as a dollar, swell day, bright, warm, makes you feel mighty proud to be alive, yes, Ma'am! There it is! You can see it now, folks. That's the Island. Outside, the pleasure boat sails around the island – two worlds are in such close proximity but worlds apart – ... See them big stone walls. Dynamite-proof, escape-proof! Thirty-five hundred men in there, folks, and lots of 'em'll never get out! Wonder what it feels like t' be locked up in a place like that 'til doomsday? Oh, oh!! There goes the band, folks! Dance on the Upper Deck!' (p. 1)

The inmates also hear this reminder of life beyond the prison walls at the beginning and end of each day. Both the idea and the reality of worlds which 'are in such close proximity but worlds apart', worlds divided not only by walls but by public apathy, are reiterated in the dialogue between inmates Swifty and Butch:

> SWIFTY: But a con's a human being. He's got to be treated like one.
>
> BUTCH: A con ain't a human being. A con's a con. He's stuck in here and the world forgot him. As far as the world's concerned he doesn't exist anymore. What happened to him in here, them people outside don't know. They don't care. He's entrusted to the care of the state. The state? Hell! The state turns him over to a guy called a warden and a bunch of other guys called guards ... (pp. 52–53)

Through this exchange and the repetition of the pleasure boat scene, Williams provokes the theatre audience to reflect on their own attitudes. He reminds them that it is one thing to be aware of prisons and the additional punishments carried out within them whenever atrocities are exposed, quite another to be aware of the actuality of prison life on an ongoing basis. Lack of care, vigilance or debate fosters a society in which prisoners are forgotten and abuse is routine.

In *Nightingales*, Williams raises questions about what can be expected of audiences and about the capabilities of theatre to elicit a critical engagement with, rather than an affective response to, the issues addressed. He uses theatre to facilitate ways of seeing, of witnessing, to support public demands that the treatment of prisoners, carried out by the state in their collective name, is truly just.

Fortune and Men's Eyes

John Herbert's *Fortune and Men's Eyes* (1967), based on his experience of a Canadian reformatory for young men, had a significant impact on the public perception of life behind bars and the lived experience of ex-prisoners. The title is a reference to William Shakespeare's Sonnet 29, which begins, 'When in disgrace with fortune and men's eyes / I all alone, beweep my outcast state ...'. The play dramatises the invidious treatment of homosexuals through sexual violence and slavery and how this is condoned by prison staff. However, it is also a testament to the possibility of small acts of care between people despite their experience of the living hell they endure under the eye of the state.

Herbert wrote the play between 1963 and 1966, a time prior to the Stonewall riots in New York (1969) which catalysed the gay rights movement within and beyond the USA, when homosexuality was illegal in most western countries, including Canada. Initially, theatre producers in Canada refused to stage the play. The criminalisation of homosexuality fostered tentative rather than explicit stage representations, but *Fortune* went further, presenting not only homosexuality but the brutality of sexual violence and the state's complicity in it. The play was considered to be too much for a Canadian theatre-going audience to handle.

Eventually *Fortune* was picked up by the New York producer David Rotherburg and ran in the Actors' Studio, New York, to popular and critical acclaim for 11 months before touring the USA and Canada in 1967–68. It fuelled a public and political debate that continued around the world, with stagings in Europe, South Africa and South America in the years immediately following the original production. To date it has been presented in more than 100 countries. *Fortune* dared to reflect a version of the world that was raw, brutalised and unjust and demanded that theatre audiences think about what happens in prison and *do* something about it.

In addition to the public debate and the critical awareness of additional punishments administered or condoned by the state within the prison system, the most significant direct response to the initial production of the play was the establishment of the Fortune Society. This New York-based charity advocates alternatives to incarceration and aims to raise public awareness of the issues facing prisoners after their release, while offering practical support to them. Institutional routine and prescribed behaviour strip many ex-prisoners of their ability and confidence to make decisions, large or small. Pragmatic considerations of where to live, how to earn money and what to eat are overwhelming, and many people find themselves living on the street, unable to rebuild their lives. Recent research in the UK evidences the vulnerability of those who have recently been released from prison: nearly 75 per cent of homeless day-centre clients have a criminal record. Among those with access to stable housing, the risk of re-offending is reduced by 20 per cent (Homeless Link, *Survey of Needs and Provision 2010*, 2010, p. 2). The Fortune Society seeks to intervene in the downward spiral towards homelessness, potential drug addiction and further criminal activity. Through education and training programmes, it supports individuals as they negotiate the transition from a world which removes independence to one which demands agency. In addition to this practical support, the Fortune Society recently launched the David Rothenberg Center for Public Policy (DRCPP), which focuses primarily on public policy advocacy for a fairer criminal justice system. *Fortune and Men's Eyes*, a play which faced considerable resistance when it was written in the late 1960s, has activated an ongoing public response and catalysed a charity which materially affects the lives of thousands of people released from prison.

These three examples illustrate that theatre can have a significant and specific impact on people's critical understanding of the ideology and practice of prison. In 1947, the Prison Commissioner, Alexander Paterson, summarised the potential of theatre as a catalyst for action in the foreword he wrote for William Douglas Home's play *Now Barabbas…* (Bolton's Theatre, London, 1947):

> [T]his play, both on the stage and in book form, [will] reach a far wider thinking public

than can ever be affected by official reports, and ... will ... focus the attention upon the prison problem. Two features of this problem [Douglas Home] has emphasised with considerable clarity and fairness. The first is that among even a small group of ten or twelve prisoners there is to be found a most bewildering variety of different types. Each man is distinct and completely different from each of the others. The only thing they have in common is that they are all in prison. This diversity, making each man a problem and a proposition by himself, illustrates the difficulty of the authorities in applying the same prison code and rules and discipline to the whole mass of four hundred or five hundred men in a single prison.

This play will do good because it will enlist the sympathy and interest of a wide circle of intelligent people, and will make them think and ask questions; and above all it should make them more ready to help men who have passed through this strange experience, and on emerging are a little dazzled by the first taste of freedom. (pp. viii–ix)

Paterson's comments about theatre's ability to reach, engage and activate an audience are as pertinent now in the globalised twenty-first century world as they were in post-war England.

Part Three

theatre in prison

The prison drama genre – on stage and screen – illustrates how the physical and metaphorical site of prison
hosts rich narrative possibilities: boredom, regret, anger,
love and desire are highly flammable emotions in a world of
containment, surveillance and routine. But the relationship
between form and content isn't one-way: a number of plays
set in a prison context use the meta-theatrical device of the
play-within-the-play to reveal something of the nature not
only of prison but of theatre itself. Michel Marc Bouchard's
Les Feluettes (National Arts Centre, Ottawa, 1987) features
a play written by an inmate who has been imprisoned for a
murder he didn't commit. It is staged before the killer, who
had escaped justice for over 40 years. In this play, theatre
is the site where the truth is seen and justice is done. Athol
Fugard's *The Island* (Space Theatre, Cape Town, 1973), set
during Apartheid, depicts the staging of a two-hander version of Sophocles' *Antigone* (Athens, 438 BC) as part of a

prison concert on Robben Island. Here, the theatrical device encourages comparison of the fracture between morality and state justice addressed in Sophocles' play with the government of South Africa at the time. In Herbert's *Fortune and Men's Eyes*, prisoners are getting ready for a prison talent show and one of the characters, Mona, prepares Portia's 'quality of mercy' speech from *The Merchant of Venice*. The optimism for justice and salvation offered by both Portia and Mona in this speech is harshly undercut by the brutality of the gang rape inflicted on Mona by his fellow inmates and of the guards who condone it. In each of these examples theatre goes beyond its narrative function, using its intrinsic nature, qualities and form to question imprisonment as a state technology of justice.

However, prisons are not only sites for imagined dramas; they have also been the stage for a wide range of theatre practice *within* the prison walls. It is this work, which occurs in many countries, including Australia, Azerbaijan, Brazil, Chile, England, Ireland, Italy, South Africa and the USA, that is the main focus of this section.

Theatre in prison practices

Prisons might appear to be unlikely theatre venues but, at this moment in time, there will be theatre projects happening in prison yards, chapels and dining rooms – spaces large enough to accommodate theatre workshops, rehearsals and performances. But what does theatre in prison look like? What forms does it take? The picture that emerges is not reducible to one model but rather comprises a wide range of practices which include theatre made by inmates for inmates, professional productions staged for prisoners, and productions with a mixed company of professional actors and prisoners which may be open to a public audience who are invited into the prison.

One of the earliest recorded examples of theatre with prisoners is the 1789 staging of George Farquhar's Restoration comedy *The Recruiting Officer* by convicts transported to found the British colony of New South Wales. This event was the catalyst for Timberlake Wertenbaker's *Our Country's Good* (Royal Court, London, 1988), which questions the value of punishment and the redemptive possibilities of theatre. There are photographic records of female impersonator competitions, minstrel shows and Christmas concerts in San Quentin, California, in the 1910s. In the early 1920s, Ossining prison in New York was the venue for previews of Broadway shows. In 1956, the San Francisco Actors' Company performed Samuel Beckett's *Waiting for Godot* (Théâtre de Babylone, Paris, 1953) at San Quentin. The play, which had recently met with derision, confusion and celebration in the public theatres of Europe and America, was warmly received by the inmates and inspired one of them, Rick Cluchey, to establish the San Quentin Drama Workshop (SQDW), the first prison theatre company. The SQDW produced more than 35 plays within the prison, many of them productions of Beckett's work. On release, Cluchey worked with Beckett, and he continues to tour his work to prisons around the world.

Also in the USA, Rhodessa Jones and Pat Graney have established long-running performance programmes especially for women, an area of work which is also pursued by Maud Clarke in Australia.

In Italy, roughly half of the country's 205 prisons have theatre programmes. In Volterra, Compagnia della Fortezza has been theatre company in residence at Fortezza Medicea maximum-security prison for over 20 years. Their eclectic canon includes Shakespeare, Bertolt Brecht and Peter Handke, and many of their productions are staged as part of the Festival VolterraTeatro.

During the 1970s and 1980s, republican political prisoners in HMP Maze, in Northern Ireland, used theatre for peer education and rigorous exploration of questions of national identity, republicanism and representation (Bill McDonnell, *Theatres of the Troubles*, 2008).

In Durban, Christopher Hurst and Miranda Young-Jahangeer have developed theatre in prison programmes which engage with the complex socio-political landscape of post-Apartheid South Africa (Young-Jahangeer, 'Working from the Inside/Out', 2004).

Over the past 30 years, the UK has seen the development of a strong tradition of theatre with prisoners and with those who are considered to be at risk of offending. One of the first extensively documented projects was a collaboration between the Royal Shakespeare Company (RSC), Royal National Theatre, Wilde Community Theatre and HMP Broadmoor, a high-security psychiatric hospital in England for people who have 'committed serious crimes whilst influenced by mental disorder and requiring long term care in a secure setting' (Murray Cox, *Shakespeare Comes to Broadmoor*, 1992, p. 17). The project, which began in 1989, grew out of conversations between theatre makers and psychiatrists at a dramatherapy conference hosted by the RSC. Currently, in the UK, Clean Break, Geese, Rideout, Escape Artists and Dance United are some of the more established companies which specialise in making performance with prisoners. Glyndebourne Opera and Pimlico Opera stage productions with mixed casts of professional actors and prisoners which are open to a public audience within prison walls, while Only Connect, Synergy and Playing Out explicitly work with ex-prisoners and professional actors to stage work in public theatre venues.

In addition to this production-based work, there is a significant body of practice using drama to address specific issues, including communication skills, human rights, parenting and resettlement. These projects articulate how theatre can be used as a creative means to a social or educative end with an emphasis on the *process* of drama and its non-arts outcomes rather than the *production* of theatre. The Theatre in Prisons and Probation (TiPP) Centre, established by Paul Heritage and James Thompson at Manchester University in 1992, developed theatre projects such as *Blagg!* and *Pump* which focused on offending behaviour and anger management. They pioneered theatre training programmes with prison and probation staff and undergraduate students, some of whom have gone on to develop theatre companies working specifically in prison. The work of TiPP has had a profound impact on the range and reach of theatre in prison practice in the UK and internationally.

Many examples of contemporary theatre in prison frame their practice though the outcomes they promise. For example, Safe Ground run accredited courses, *Family Man* and *Fathers Inside*, which use storytelling and drama as ways to support parents in prison to engage with their children's learning and continue to develop family relationships despite the rupture to everyday familial life. Clean Break's *Miss Spent* is a theatre and visual arts programme with young female offenders and those considered to be at risk of offending. It is an accredited personal development course whose participants can be entered for the 'Working with Others' award, part of the Department for Children, Schools and Families' Key Skills Qualification, which outlines skills required to promote success in education, employment and personal development. Playing for Time is a theatre company based at the University of Winchester which develops collaborations between students and prisoners. The company's website highlights the 'transferable skills that accrue to this process such as the enhancement of self-confidence and esteem, team building, communication and self-presentation skills' (www.playingfortime.org.uk).

Each of these examples is described in terms of its intentions to develop, through participation in drama, specific educational and social impacts in the future. This framing and accounting presents theatre in prison practice as a process with predetermined outcomes: the participants will achieve these learnings; they will gain these skills.

This articulation of its value has advanced the profession-alisation of theatre in prison practice over the past two decades. However, this success has also been a limitation as, increasingly, theatre in prison practice is referred to in terms only of the predefined outcomes it promises and its success in keeping those promises. Theatre makers working in prison are asked 'Does it work? Does theatre increase communication skills, and therefore employability, with a subsequent reduction in crime?' much more frequently than they are asked about the aesthetic or political terrain of their work. This has had a practical and critical impact on theatre in prison which I will expand on in the section 'The Application of Theatre in Prison Contexts'.

Over the past decade, while working as a practitioner and academic in this area, I have been aware of assumptions that this work has a particular kind of left-leaning politics and that theatre in prison is a radical performance prac-tice because it is *in* a prison. The authority of the prison building, as a manifestation of the state's power to detain and punish, is seen to be ideologically compromised by the artist's act of border crossing. But performance practice in prisons cannot be assumed either to be left-leaning or to be radical. The site alone, or the constituency of participants, does not make the work radical. This claim can be made only of the methodology. In the following section I want to consider specific examples of theatre in prison, from pro-duction-based work in the early twentieth century through to contemporary applied performance practice, in order to consider particular methodological approaches and how they engage with, challenge or are complicit in the ideology and practice of prisons.

Theatre and prison: immiscible worlds

The worlds of theatre and prison appear immiscible. On a very basic level, prisons are places associated with punishment and pain, and theatres are places associated with entertainment and pleasure. However, both sites are culturally defined spaces which reflect, re-inscribe or, potentially, re-imagine ways of being in the world. They negotiate the relationship between the individual, the audience/community and, thence, the state. Both contexts and practices raise pertinent questions about the use of time and space, narratives of possibility, intentionality and audience.

The smooth administration of prison depends on the strict demarcation of time, space and action: particular behaviours happen in specific places for an allocated duration. People are assigned roles which are hierarchical, segregated and fixed; within this context a prisoner is always a prisoner and a guard is always a guard. Irregularities and surprises are not welcome; they are risks to be avoided, flaws which interrupt the institutional machine. Surety and certainty are the foundations upon which the prison world is built. The prison administration is monitored to ensure that it performs, that targets are reached and that the audience – the government department responsible for prisons – is satisfied its expectations have been met.

In contrast, theatre demands a provocation of ideas of certainty. It invites a playful exploration of time, space and action. In theatre, we expect that people and objects might *not* be what they appear to be: an actor can play a young woman, an older man, a child or a thing; the same table can become an island, a cave or a pulpit. Time jumps from the present to the past to the future. A narrative which unfolds over three decades of experience can be told in an hour or represented in a minute. In the theatre, we play with the truth. Deception is welcomed. Audiences are expected to navigate their way between the world they physically live in and the fantasy world of the stage with imaginative dexterity. Inventiveness and fluidity of meaning are embraced.

Disruptions

Theatre in prison heightens the distinctions between these two worlds. In this section I consider two examples of theatre in prison which reveal the capacity of theatre to quietly disrupt the institutional machine and work with individual criminal bodies in ways which expose the performance of certainty in the prison routine and its seemingly stable referents of time, space, action and role.

Disruption 1: Sarah Bernhardt, San Quentin, 1913

One of the earliest recorded examples of theatre in prison is Sarah Bernhardt's visit to San Quentin prison in California in 1913. The legendary stage and screen star performed an extract from *Une Nuit de Noël* with her company on her final tour of America. This event was reported on the front page of the *Spartanburg Herald-Journal* under the heading 'Sarah Bernhardt Pleases Convicts – Her Company Gives

Performance in French for 2,000 Prisoners in San Quentin'
(22 February 1913). I include the full details of the report as
it provokes useful questions about ideas of theatre in prison
which are as potent today as they were nearly a century ago.

> For their Washington's birthday holiday the
> 2,000 prisoners of San Quentin were entertained
> by a company of French players, who appeared
> on a rough stage in the prison yard.
>
> Although the play was in a foreign tongue,
> the convicts followed eagerly every word and
> gesture and they were particularly interested in
> the work of Mme. Sarah Bernhardt, who was
> one of the actresses.
>
> An impressive scene followed the entertain-
> ment. A tall gray-haired prisoner, a Frenchman,
> stepped from the wings and bowed to the play-
> ers. He then read in French a testimonial from
> the prison inmates written by Abe Ruef, the
> political boss, convicted by the San Francisco
> graft prosecution.
>
> 'Today for an hour,' the old Frenchman read,
> 'these stone walls have faded away. For an hour
> your great art has made us free. Our hearts have
> been touched by the actors and the play. We
> extend to you our grateful thanks.'

Superficially, this event can be read purely as entertainment
for prisoners and prison staff. This one-off event, a celebrity

appearance in the prison yard on a winter's morning, is institutionally sanctioned, providing distraction from the relentless routine of prison life and contributing to the smooth running of the machine. However, it can also be read as an act of disruption which challenges concepts of time, space and the materiality of the prison world. The federal holiday already interrupts the monotony of the prison calendar. Bernhardt's performance is a double disruption: facilitating access to the prison for a theatre troupe and supporting their performance would have required considerable negotiation within the senior prison management. The prison yard, usually a site of association and exercise, becomes, through the building of the 'rough stage', an outdoor theatre space where the certainty of prison life is ruptured and previously unimagined worlds are offered. For those who have witnessed the performance, in the weeks, months and years following Bernhardt's appearance, the prison yard will no longer be just the prison yard: it will be configured as a place of other possibilities.

This report also raises questions about the language that is used to describe theatre as a transformative, liberating and dignifying encounter within a prison context. 'These stone walls have faded away', 'your great art has made us free' and 'our hearts have been touched by the actors and the play' might appear to be sentimental in an environment which is notoriously brutal. However, they hint at the transporting shifts that theatre invites of its audience. The event also reframes the identity and perception of the mass group of prisoners. Two thousand bodies which were usually segregated and separated in different areas of the prison were brought together to watch a play in a language most would not have understood. This performance transformed the prisoners – in the eyes of the prisoners themselves, the actors and the newspaper reporter – from a group of criminal bodies into a theatre audience who behaved as such. Just as the institutional conventions of the prison inform the behaviour of those who live and work within it, the expectations that are made of a theatre audience inflect the actions of those who attend. The layering of the theatre space upon the prison meant that the two sets of conventions were negotiated; the everyday rules of the prison, while not obliterated, were circumvented by the theatre. The stone walls remain and the men are still incarcerated. However, the disturbance of the theatre event allows moments of parallel alternatives to be imagined and realised.

Disruption 2: Split Britches, HMP Highpoint, 2002

From 2002 to 2004, Lois Weaver and Peggy Shaw of Split Britches and I worked with women in prison in England and Brazil as part of the *Staging Human Rights* programme. (I will discuss the overall framework for *Staging Human Rights* in more detail later.) Weaver and Shaw led the residencies, and I was the researcher, documenting and critically witnessing the work.

Weaver and Shaw's approach to making theatre with women in prison reflects their own devising process, working with impulse, imagination and fantasy, found objects, obsessions and desires. Characters emerge from a bricolage of material, fusing personal experience, fantastical imaginings, current affairs and half-remembered stories. Each residency in the programme shared this approach to making work but had no predetermined outcome of form or content.

At the beginning of every session we would do a series of warm-up exercises. Simple movements such as gently shaking a hand or a leg or articulating the shoulder or hip joint would result in loud groans of discomfort or surprise as these institutionalised bodies, which had had a limited range of everyday movements, were encouraged to find new ways of moving. This prompted the women to speak about their bodies and the uneasy relationship they had with them in prison: they were lethargic with medication and heavier with prison food, and their skin was grey from lack of sunlight. Their sense of themselves, of their own bodies, was impacted by the routine of the institution. The sense of a de-limited body was reiterated during another exercise in which each of the women had written a story which featured her fantasy character – a composite of 'what if' possibilities.

> Lois chooses one of the stories we have just heard and reads it out to the group. She then invites the group to mould her body, to create a statue, a portrait of the character in the story. She offers her body as a piece of malleable but delicate clay and invites the group to consider what they have heard and to gently shape and manipulate her

body. They can make facial expressions for her to mirror, they can give her props to illustrate her character. The group tentatively approach Lois. Yes, she is the theatre woman who is visiting them, who has made them laugh, who has helped them make these stories but she is also a figure of authority. The teacher. Can they really touch and manipulate her body? Gradually and with increasing confidence as it becomes clear that their actions won't warrant punishment, the women shape Lois's body. When they are satisfied, they step back. Lois holds the pose, a physical portrait of one of the characters created by the group. The group are happy with the likeness they have made. Lois then invites them to get into small groups to set about modelling each other. The women take the same level of care and attention when modelling each other as they did when working with Lois. (McAvinchey, Possible Fictions, 2007, pp. 181–82)

By offering herself as a model for the group, by literally putting herself in the group's hands, Lois articulates both her trust in the group and the expectation she has of the group to take responsibility for her and for each other. In a world where bodies are segregated and touch is prohibited, this particular approach to making theatre creates a parallel world and permissible opportunity where the usual rules do not apply. Behaviour that would not ordinarily be permitted, that would be punished, was condoned within the parameters of theatre.

Neither of these examples of theatre in prison declared itself as having the intention to interrogate the ideology of incarceration: the former was presented as entertainment for a whole prison and the latter as a workshop with a small number of women by visiting artists. But both theatre interventions exposed the fragility of the institutional rules, gently disrupting the routine and exposing its impact on those whose lives are governed by it.

Dialogues of reform

In this section I want to consider two examples of theatre as an agent of reform advocated for *within* a prison system. Once again, these are two very different models of practice in different cultural and historical contexts.

Dialogues of reform 1: Broadway goes to Sing Sing

The first is described by a report published in the *New York Times* in April 1921:

> A year ago the Entertainment Committee of the Mutual Welfare Association at Sing Sing put on two little dramas, together with a vaudeville and musical entertainment, one for the men themselves, and later for three public performances in the prison. It is the job of the Entertainment Committee to keep the men out of their cells as late into the evening as possible, and for this

purpose it gives nightly a motion picture entertainment interspersed with vaudeville numbers
and short plays.

There was only one place where these enter-
tainments could be held and that was the Chapel.
The Drama League brought the attention of
David Belasco to the meagre equipment of the
prison, and Mr. Belasco sent a small staff of
assistants – property man, scenic artist, machin-
ist, electrician, &c, – to the prison. These men
studied the conditions and arranged to build a
stage on which simple plays could be produced.
The actual result has been a well-equipped,
portable stage. This stage was designed by Mr.
Garson of Mr. Belasco's staff. The first performance was held on the evening of Dec. 26, when
Brock Pemberton presented 'Miss Lulu Bett' for
the first time on any stage. Since then three or
four companies from New York have given performances in the Sing Sing theatre. ('Drama in
Prison Reform', *New York Times*, 3 April 1921)

There are a number of extraordinary things raised in this
newspaper report that require contextualisation. David
Belasco was a theatre writer, producer and impresario who
owned and managed two theatres in New York's Times
Square. He donated a stage, four sets and an array of theatre lamps to Sing Sing. Between 1914 and 1921, Sing Sing
prison, under the management of the wardens Thomas

Mott Osborne and Lewis E. Lawes, hosted a number of professional productions, including previews of Broadway productions. These performances were usually presented to the prisoners as part of the prison's Christmas celebrations. *Miss Lulu Bett* was an adaptation of the best-selling novel by Zona Gale about the life of a single woman in the Midwest – her choices, ambitions and decisions. The play opened in the Belmont Theatre, Broadway, in 1944, the day after its premiere in Sing Sing, and won Gale the Pulitzer Prize for Drama – the first for a female dramatist. In a contemporary context, this would be the equivalent of Cameron Mackintosh overseeing the construction of a stage in HMP Wormwood Scrubs and previewing a new West End production there. This would cause a political and public outcry from those who consider prison to be a place of punishment where prisoners are reformed through austerity rather than education or rehabilitation. Such a reaction was evident in the tabloid furore that erupted about stand-up comedy workshops in HMP Whitemoor in November 2008, which resulted in the then Justice Secretary, Jack Straw, banning this activity.

The newspaper quotation is from a story about the 1921 New York Drama League conference, which discussed many issues relating to theatre – from children's theatre to 'The Relation of Drama to Prison Reform'. This section of the conference was led by Osborne and Lawes, who, despite their authority as prison wardens, had faced considerable political and practical opposition to their ideas of penal reform. They argued that the existing prison system infantilised prisoners by removing choice, independence and all traces of ordinary, everyday life. Prison could, they proposed, offer inmates a genuine opportunity to reform if the system treated them as people who would, given the opportunity and support, take responsibility for themselves and others.

In the early twentieth century there was a growing penal reform movement in the USA and the UK: while Galsworthy was writing plays promoting the need for social justice for prisoners, Osborne and Lawes were persuading professional theatre producers to present work in prison as part of an internal campaign to re-imagine the rationale for incarceration. In this context, theatre was not only an entertainment to keep the prisoners engaged in the evenings, a distraction from boredom and routine and a means of keeping the peace; it was also a commitment to treating convicts as people with the same needs, interests, desires and cultural appetites as those who lived beyond the prison walls. Although inmates no longer had their liberty, Osborne and Lawes argued that prison should not be a place of further social and cultural deprivation. Rather, prison should be a place of growth, development and reform and theatre a social, political and cultural activity that would aid this realisation.

Nearly a century later, in the vast Brazilian city of São Paulo, the country's Minister for Justice and senior prison administration staff were engaged in a similar conversation. Could theatre be used as a means to catalyse penal reform across Brazil's federal system?

Dialogues of reform 2: *Staging Human Rights*

Staging Human Rights was a performance project addressing human rights issues with those who lived and worked in the adult prison system in Brazil. It was initiated by Paul Heritage and delivered through People's Palace Projects (PPP), a non-governmental organisation and applied performance research unit at Queen Mary, University of London. Heritage and James Thompson have written extensively about this work, but it is important to include it in this book as it is a rare example of theatre in prison seeking to provoke ideological critique and institutional change by working not just with prisoners but with prison staff.

Staging Human Rights was not an interventionist act which sought to uncover and condemn human rights abuses within prisons. Rather, it was an attempt to engage those who lived and worked in prisons in a conversation about human rights. What are they? What do they mean in the context of a notoriously inhumane system? What articulations of human rights fall beyond the words and between the lines of the United Nations Universal Declaration of Human Rights? Whose responsibility are they? Is it possible to re-imagine and reconfigure a system that has been ruptured by a history of human rights abuses?

Funded by a range of partners, including the Brazilian Ministry of Justice, the programme worked with prison education workers, training them in the participatory drama techniques of Augusto Boal. The staff then returned to their institution and initiated conversations, through theatre, about human rights with guards and prisoners. These conversations culminated in forum theatre performances, called 'dialogues', within the prison with prison staff and prisoners. After a series of dialogues, each prison was expected to stage a Public Forum where members of the public were invited to the prison to interact with the theatre forums. Some prisons took their plays beyond the prison walls to town squares, opening this conversation to wider civic society. The first phase of *Staging Human Rights* culminated at the Latin American Parliament in São Paulo on 12 December 2001. An audience of lawyers, prison guards, prisoners, their families, human rights workers and the Secretaries of Justice and Prison Administration gathered to reflect and act upon the conversations that had been staged over the previous year.

What can be seen as, on one level, a simple theatre workshop in a room in a prison suddenly becomes a state-wide interruption of the institutional routine, condoned *by* the institution. The reforming ambition for the project was that small shifts in attitude and action in everyday encounters might, over time, become inscribed within the individual and institutional memory, enabling a cultural shift. If a new language of human rights, based on a shared concern for the everyday dignity of, and respect for, each individual, could be created and articulated *by* those individuals, then the language of human rights could be liberated from the realm of accusation and condemnation. As Tim Etchells succinctly states, 'It works small, the history thing. Small things make big changes' (*Certain Fragments*, 1999, p. 19).

Both these examples, from Sing Sing and São Paulo, evidence how theatre has been used as a way to provoke thinking about the ideology of prison from within the prison walls. They illustrate the need for dialogue about penal reform to be led by or negotiated with the leaders of institutions who have the authority to set a tone and to reframe a regime so that it is mindful of its impact on prisoners, prison staff and how the function of prison is perceived in the world beyond its walls.

The application of theatre in prison contexts: an economic and political concern

The final area of theatre work I will consider is a recent trend in practice in which theatre methodologies are applied to educative and social problems associated with crime. This work provokes critical questions about the political and economic frameworks which support crime and about ideas of activism within the criminal justice system.

There have been two distinct phases in the development in the USA and the UK of theatre work which seeks to address social issues of crime and punishment: from the 1960s to the 1980s and from the 1990s to the 2010s. In the USA, during the 1960s, the civil rights movements catalysed the prisoners' rights movement. Activists argued that even though prisoners had had their liberty removed, this should not mean that basic human rights were neglected or abused. Calls for equality, dignity and humanity prompted shifts within the prison system: progressive education, meaningful activity and training were seen as rehabilitative practices that would impact prisoners' experience within and beyond the prison. Individual volunteers and charities provided time and expertise to support reform through informal arts educational programmes. For example, Alan Mandell, an actor in the production of *Godot* at San Quentin (1956), volunteered to work in the prison for more than seven years after this event, and the actor and director Marvin Felix Camillo worked with prisoners in Sing Sing and Bedford Hills Correctional Facility, some of whom, on their release, formed The Family, Inc. theatre company during the 1970s. By the late 1970s, California's Department of Corrections had included arts programmes in its annual budget.

These examples illustrate distinct areas of progressive thinking about the arts in individual institutions rather than a national strategy. There were many people who failed to be convinced of the propriety or value of the arts in corrections:

> If things are made … pleasant for convicts … the result will be that the decent, law-abiding citizens are paying the bill to give enjoyments to convicts which many of them have not the money to buy for themselves. Instead of being made pleasant and enjoyable, life … should be made so terrible that when the convict comes out he will say: 'The punishment for crime is so terrible, let's all be good.' ('Police Disapprove Osborne's Sing Sing', *New York Times*, 18 May 1915)

This quotation from Second Deputy Commissioner Frank A. Lord, commenting on theatre projects in Sing Sing prison in the early 1900s, continues to resonate today. To counter such an attitude, anecdotal evidence needed to be re-presented in a way which spoke to both the financial and the political concerns of sceptics.

One of the earliest attempts to evaluate the social and economic impact of the arts in prisons was made in 1983 by Lawrence Brewster, a political scientist, on behalf of the California Department of Corrections and the William James Association, which initiated the Prison Arts Project (PAP). Although Brewster observed four multidisciplinary arts programmes rather than theatre-specific programmes, the terms and detail of his findings inform our understanding of the politics and economics of theatre in prison.

Brewster attempted to develop a cost–benefit analysis of the Arts-in-Corrections programme in California. He identified an economic price for delivering the arts programme and for the qualitative, social benefits of the arts within the prison. He defined the social benefits as direct services to inmates, reduced institutional tension, cost avoidance, institutional enrichment and community service, and he gave each of these categories an economic value. His study proposed that the cost of the programme was $123,110 and that the economic value of the social benefits was $228,522. This financial model, which illustrates the social return on investment (SROI) of the arts in the penal context, made a business case for the benefits of the art to the prison – its inmates, staff and working environment – and its relationship with the community through increased connections and understandings (*An Evaluation of the Arts-in-Corrections Programme of the California Department of Corrections*, 1983, p. 1). This discourse of investment and return directly reflects capitalist models of operation in private management, which are increasingly being used in the public sector. In Brewster's work, the arts are seen as being of value in the present tense, in the living and work-ing environment, in relationships between people and in the material conditions of the prison. This language and political concern is very different from that since the 1990s, when much theatre in prison in the UK and the USA has been framed and funded as intended to contribute to *future* crime reduction by tackling offenders' behaviour, particu-larly rates of recidivism.

In the UK, this language of social exclusion and inclu-sion was rooted in the cultural and social policies of the 1997–2010 Labour government. In 1997, it established the Social Exclusion Unit, which attempted to think across gov-ernment departments by establishing Policy Action Teams (PATs). The positive findings of PAT 10 – the team respon-sible for considering the impact of sports and arts on issues of social inclusion – combined with François Matarasso's persuasive report *Use or Ornament? The Social Impact of Participation in the Arts* (1997), informed the development of policies and subsequent funding streams to support arts work which addressed social issues of exclusion and crime. Some arts organisations, such as Geese Theatre Company and TiPP, which had been developing work in this area for some time found that they had new sources of funding available. Other arts organisations which had no track record of working in the criminal justice system designed projects which would satisfy funding requirements. Towards the end of the 1990s and through the 2000s, the Arts in Prison directory – a compilation of arts organisations working in the criminal justice system in the UK published by the Unit for Arts and Offenders – expanded dramatically, reflecting the growth in the business of arts activity in the criminal justice system.

But this *business* of theatre in prison needs to be recognised as such. The terms of engagement for artists working in prisons today are very different from those of the 1960s and 1970s, when many artists volunteered their time and skills, contributing to an idea of society which acknowledged prison within it. The professionalisation of the arts throughout the 1990s and 2000s saw a booming creative industry in which artists were contracted and paid to run specific programmes of work which delivered pre-identified aims and objectives aligned to those of the prison service and wider government concerns.

The pioneering, radical spirit which characterised early theatre in prison work has, in some cases, been compromised by the impact of private management principles embraced by government which inform the discourse and practice of both the arts and the criminal justice system. This was made starkly clear to me when, in discussion with a prison about a potential theatre project, I was asked to present a business plan to the governor outlining the aims and objectives of the project and how it supported those of the institution. Economy, efficiency and effectiveness are measured by target setting, monitoring and evaluation. Andrew Miles and Rebecca Clarke's feasibility study of *The Arts in Criminal Justice* highlights the impact of this vocabulary and how it 'has led to the Prisons and Probation Service having to meet the demands of a results-oriented culture, one driven by centrally determined aims and quantitative measures of performance' (2006, p. 13). But what does it mean for prisons to perform well? Her Majesty's Prison Service states that its mission is to serve

> the public by keeping in custody those committed by the courts. Our duty is to look after them with humanity and help them lead law-abiding and useful lives in custody and after release.

Interestingly, punishment isn't referred to at all. The emphasis is on rehabilitation and preparation for life after prison, where, it is hoped, people won't re-offend. The performance of prison is measured in terms of what ex-prisoners *don't* do – that is, commit crime. However, as discussed earlier, rates of recidivism of 60–70 per cent would suggest that prison as rehabilitation doesn't work. This is not a new phenomenon, and it is one that the prison service has, since the 1970s, tried to address by developing a tailored approach using cognitive behavioural therapeutic methods to address offenders' actions (Miles and Clarke, *The Arts in Criminal Justice*, p. 14). This approach is evidenced in the proliferation of offence-focused theatre projects which explicitly state that they will address and correct such unwanted acts. It is a big promise to make on behalf of theatre and of individuals that, to put it crudely, participation in a theatre project will influence someone's choice of whether or not to commit further crime when released. This claim harks back to the early days of the prison as a penitentiary – a liminal space where character was transformed through self-awareness – and to criminological theories of volunteerism which posit that crime is a choice rather than a result of complex interrelated social, political and personal circumstance *and* individual choice. This critique of applied theatre practice in prisons is not saying that it, or government agendas, are necessarily bad. However, it is calling for a critical awareness of the politics and economics of this practice, the funding bodies which support it and the institutions which enable it.

Throughout this book I have argued that rather than being benign, enduring institutions which detain criminals and protect society, prisons are the ideological manifestation of the political, social and economic values society ascribes to bodies which are seen to be culturally or legally deviant. Representations of prisons and prisoners may saturate our cultural landscape, but our familiarity with them numbs our critical consideration of them. However, as the use of incarceration continues to rise globally and as private companies are employed to build and manage the state business of punishment, we cannot afford *not* to think about the multi-billion-pound corrections industry, the value of the lives pawned within it and the relationship between the individual and the state. Thinking about theatre *and* prison offers us insights into the role of prison in narratives of justice and how we respond to our role as critical witnesses to this. Theatre offers many different interventions into the prison system – both directly and indirectly – but these actions do not necessarily share the same politics. Some practices seek to interrogate and critique the ideology and practice of prison, while some, in their casual complicity with institutional and governmental agendas, fail to acknowledge the wider political and economic landscape in which their work is enmeshed. *Theatre & Prison* is a provocation to reconsider these relationships.

Afterword

At the time of writing, winter 2010, the UK's newly established Conservative–Liberal Democrat coalition government announced extensive and painful public spending cuts in its attempt to address recession and the country's budget deficit. For years, prison reformers have lobbied government, arguing that the social and economic cost of prison is too high a price to pay for a penal practice which has been proven, since its inception over 200 years ago, not to 'work'. This argument has consistently fallen on stony ground, until now.

In a speech made in autumn 2010, the Justice Secretary, Kenneth Clarke, declared that prison, particularly for short-term sentencing, is 'a costly and ineffectual approach that fails' and that alternatives should increasingly be used.

It may be that this position will not gain traction and that the coalition, sensing a media and public backlash, will beat a hasty retreat. However, there is a dark irony here. It is possible that the very same neoliberal capitalist model which has led to global recession, the very same model that has entrenched societal structural disadvantage, has, in its moment of crisis, enabled a new era of dialogue about the ideology and practice of prison in the twenty-first century.

further reading

Outsiders' access to theatre in prison is mediated by artists, companies and scholars who have undertaken or accompanied work in secure custodial contexts, and there is a small but growing literature about performance and prison.

Murray Cox's *Shakespeare Comes to Broadmoor* (1992) was the first book to extensively address theatre practice within a secure setting, raising pertinent and difficult questions about crime, punishment, care and health. James Thompson's *Prison Theatre* (1998) and Michael Balfour's *Theatre in Prison* (2004) are edited collections of essays by theatre makers that provide insight into a range of practices in different cultural contexts during the 1990s and early 2000s. Paul Heritage has written extensively about his work in the Brazilian prison system in chapters including 'Real Social Ties?' (2002) and 'Stealing Kisses' (2004). Further information about the *Staging Human Rights* programme can be found on the People's Palace Projects website, www. peoplespalace.org.uk. Amy Scott-Douglass and Rena Fraden are academics who act as contextualising witnesses, reporting respectively on the work of the Shakespeare Behind Bars project in Kentucky and Rhodessa Jones's work with African American women in the state of California. Jenny Hughes's *Doing the Arts Justice* (2005) is an invaluable critical survey of arts practice in prison in the UK at the beginning of the twenty-first century.

Dwight Conquergood's article 'Lethal Theatre' (2002) was the first to bring the performativity of punishment well into the foreground. Although it does not deal explicitly with theatre in prison, James Thompson's most recent book, *Performance Affects* (2009), is a welcome and valuable challenge to think how applied theatre can be theoretically and politically reconsidered to be more than the sum of its assumed or prescribed outcomes.

There is an abundance of publications through which to pursue the history and practice of prisons. A good place to start is *The Oxford History of the Prison* edited by Morris and Rothman (1997), which offers a wonderfully eclectic array of essays detailing developments in the idea and practice of prisons in western society. Michel Foucault's *Discipline and Punish* (1977), an exposition of the development of the idea of the prison and of how this was implicitly linked to the development of forms of rationality, subjectivity and control, is a key text which has informed much recent writing about prisons. If you are interested in architecture, Robin Evan's *The Fabrication of Virtue: English Prison Architecture, 1750–1840* (1992) is an extraordinary book which details how shifts in design reflected penal philosophy and cultural politics. David Garland (*Punishment and Modern Society*, 1990; *Mass Imprisonment*, 2001) and Michael Ignatieff (*A Just Measure of Pain*, 1978) have contributed pivotal work on the sociology of punishment.

Ash, Juliet. *Dress Behind Bars: Prison Clothing as Criminality*. London: I.B. Tauris, 2010.

Baim, Clark, Sally Brookes, and Alun Mountford. *The Geese Theatre Handbook: Drama with Offenders and People at Risk*. Hook, UK: Waterside, 2002.

Balfour, Michael. *The Use of Drama in the Rehabilitation of Violent Male Offenders*. New York: Edwin Mellen, 2003.

———, ed. *Theatre in Prison: Theory and Practice*. Bristol: Intellect, 2004.

Beccaria, Cesare. *On Crimes and Punishment and Other Writings*. Cambridge: Cambridge UP, 1995.

Bender, John. *Imagining the Penitentiary: Fiction and the Architecture of the Mind in Eighteenth-Century England.* Chicago: U of Chicago P, 1987.

Brewster, Larry. *An Evaluation of the Arts-in-Corrections Program of the California Department of Corrections.* Report prepared for the William James Association, California, and California Department of Corrections, 1983.

Christie, Nils. *A Suitable Amount of Crime.* London: Routledge, 2004.

Churchill, Caryl. *Softcops. Plays Two.* London: Methuen, 1990.

Conquergood, Dwight. 'Lethal Theatre: Performance, Punishment and the Death Penalty.' *Theatre Journal* 54.3 (2002): 339–67.

Cox, Murray, ed. *Shakespeare Comes to Broadmoor: 'The Actors Are Come Hither': The Performance of Tragedy in a Secure Psychiatric Hospital.* London: Jessica Kingsley, 1992.

Douglas Home, William, *Now Barabbas …* London: Longmans, Green, 1947.

Dowling, Kevin. '4,300: How Labour Has Created a New Crime Every Day since 1997.' *The Times* 14 March 2010.

'Drama in Prison Reform.' *New York Times* 3 April 1921.

Equality and Human Rights Commission. *How Fair Is Britain?* London: Author, 2010.

Etchells, Tim. *Certain Fragments: Contemporary Performance and Forced Entertainment.* London: Routledge, 1999.

Evans, Robin. *The Fabrication of Virtue: English Prison Architecture, 1750–1840.* Cambridge: Cambridge UP, 1982.

Foucault, Michel. *Discipline and Punish.* Trans. Alan Sheridan. London: Penguin, 1977.

Fraden, Rena. *Imagining Medea: Rhodessa Jones and Theatre for Incarcerated Women.* Chapel Hill: U of North Carolina P, 1994.

Fugard, Athol. *The Island. The Township Plays.* Oxford: Oxford Paperbacks, 1993.

Galsworthy, John. *Justice. Five Plays.* London: Methuen, 1999.

Garland, David. *Mass Imprisonment: Social Causes and Consequences.* London: Sage, 2001.

———. *Punishment and Modern Society: A Study in Social Theory.* Oxford: Oxford UP, 1990.

Gindin, James. *John Galsworthy's Life and Art: An Alien's Fortress.* Ann Arbor: U of Michigan P, 1987.

Graney, Pat, ed. *Writings from Women on the Inside.* Seattle, WA: Author, 2003.

Grayling, A. C. *Ideas That Matter: A Personal Guide for the 21st Century.* London: Weidenfeld & Nicolson, 2009.

Gupta, Tanika. *Gladiator Games.* London: Oberon, 2005.

Herbert, John. *Fortune and Men's Eyes.* New York: Grove, 1968.

Heritage, Paul. 'Real Social Ties? The Ins and Outs of Making Theatre in Brazilian Prisons.' *Theatre in Prison: Theory and Practice.* Ed. Michael Balfour. Bristol: Intellect, 2004. 189–202.

————. 'Stealing Kisses.' *Theatre in Crisis: Performance Manifestos for a New Century.* Ed. Maria Delgado and Caridad Svich. Manchester: Manchester UP, 2002. 166–78.

————. 'Taking Hostages.' *TDR: The Drama Review* 48.3 (2004): 96–106.

Homeless Link. *Survey of Needs and Provision 2010: Criminal Justice Findings.* London: Author, 2010.

Howard, John. *The State of the Prisons.* Facsimile reprint of first edition, Warrington, 1777. Abingdon: Professional, 1977.

Hughes, Jenny. *Doing the Arts Justice: A Review of Research Literature, Practice and Theory.* Canterbury, UK: Unit for the Arts and Offenders, 2005.

Ignatieff, Michael. *A Just Measure of Pain: The Penitentiary in the Industrial Revolution.* London: Macmillan, 1978.

International Centre for Prison Studies. *World Prison Brief.* 8 November 2010 <www.kcl.ac.uk/depsta/law/research/icps/worldbrief>.

Kander, John, and Fred Ebb. *Kiss of the Spider Woman.* Milwaukee, WI: Hal Leonard, 2004.

Kander, John, Fred Ebb, and Bob Fosse. *Chicago: A Musical Vaudeville.* London: International Music Publications, 2003.

Lee Adams, William. 'Norway Builds the World's Most Humane Prison.' *Time Magazine* 10 May 2010.

Linebaugh, Peter. *The London Hanged: Crime and Civil Society in the Eighteenth Century.* London: Verso, 2006.

Locke, John. *An Essay Concerning Human Understanding.* Oxford: Oxford UP, 2008.

Matarasso, François. *Use or Ornament? The Social Impact of Participation in the Arts.* Stroud, UK: Comedia, 1997.

McAvinchey, Caoimhe. Possible Fictions: The Testimony of Applied Performance with Women in Prison in England and Brazil. PhD thesis, Queen Mary, U of London, 2007.

McDonnell, Bill. *Theatres of the Troubles: Theatre, Resistance, and Liberation in Ireland.* Exeter: U of Exeter P, 2008.

McLaughlin, Eugene, John Muncie, and Gordon Hughes, eds. *Criminological Perspectives: Essential Readings.* London: Sage, 2003.

Miles, Andrew, and Rebecca Clarke. *The Arts in Criminal Justice: A Study of Research Feasibility.* Manchester: Centre for Research on Socio-Cultural Change, U of Manchester, 2006.

Ministry of Justice. 'Reoffending of Adults: Results from 2008 Cohort.' *Ministry of Justice Statistics Bulletin* 18 March 2010. London: Author, 2010.

Morgan, Rod, and Alison Liebling. 'Imprisonment: An Expanding Scene.' *The Oxford Handbook of Criminology*. Ed. Mike Maguire, Rod Morgan, and Robert Reiner. Oxford: Oxford UP, 2007. 1100–38.

Morris, Norval, and David J. Rothman, eds. *The Oxford History of the Prison: The Practice of Punishment in Western Society*. Oxford: Oxford UP, 1997.

Munro, Rona. *Iron*. London: Nick Hern, 2002.

Piñero, Miguel. *Short Eyes*. New York: Hill and Wang, 1975.

'Police Disapprove Osborne's Sing Sing.' *New York Times* 18 May 1915.

Prison Reform Trust. *Private Punishment: Who Profits?* London: Author, 2005.

Ruck, S. K., ed. *Paterson on Prisons. The Collected Papers of Sir Alexander Paterson*. London: Frederick Muller, 1951.

Rusche, George, and Otto Kirchheimer. *Punishment and Social Structure*. New York: Columbia UP, 1939.

'Sarah Bernhardt Pleases Convicts – Her Company Gives Performance in French for 2,000 Prisoners in San Quentin.' *Spartanburg Herald-Journal* 22 February 1913.

Scott-Douglass, Amy. *Shakespeare Inside: The Bard Behind Bars*. London: Continuum, 2007.

Spierenburg, Pieter. 'The Body and the State: Early Modern Europe.' *The Oxford History of the Prison: The Practice of Punishment in Western Society*. Ed. Norval Morris and David J. Rothman. Oxford: Oxford UP, 1997. 44–70.

Stern, Vivien. *Bricks of Shame: Britain's Prisons*. New York: Penguin, 1987.

———. *Creating Criminals: Prisons and People in a Market Society*. London: Zed, 2006.

———. *A Sin against the Future: Imprisonment in the World*. Boston: Northeastern UP, 1998.

Thompson, James. *Drama Workshops for Anger Management and Offending Behaviour*. London: Jessica Kingsley, 1999.

———. *Performance Affects: Applied Theatre and the End of Effect*. Basingstoke: Palgrave Macmillan, 2009.

———, ed. *Prison Theatre: Perspectives and Practices*. London: Jessica Kingsley, 1998.

Trounstine, Jean. *Shakespeare Behind Bars: One Teacher's Story of the Power of Drama in Women's Prison*. Ann Arbor: U of Michigan P, 2004.

Watkins, Maurine Dallas. *Chicago, or, Play Ball*. New York: Knopf, 1927.

Weaver, Lois. 'Doing Time: A Personal and Practical Account of Making Performance Work in Prisons.' *The Applied Theatre Reader*. Ed. Sheila Preston and Tim Prentki. London: Routledge, 2008. 55–61.

Wertenbaker, Timberlake. *Our Country's Good*. London: Methuen, 1988.

Williams, Tennessee. *Not About Nightingales*. London: Methuen, 1998.

Wilson, David, and Sean O'Sullivan. *Images of Incarceration: Representations of Prison in Film and Television Drama*. Winchester, UK: Waterside, 2004.

Young-Jahangeer, Miranda. 'Working from the Inside/Out: Drama as Activism in Westville Female Prison.' *Pan African Issues in Crime and Justice*. Ed. Anita Kalunta-Crumpton and Biko Agozino. Aldershot, UK: Ashgate, 2004. 136–56.

Materials published by particular companies, such as websites, education packs and project evaluations, offer us some further insights into this work:

Clean Break Theatre Company: www.cleanbreak.org.uk.

Dance United: www.dance-united.com.

Escape Artists: www.escapeartists.co.uk.

Geese Theatre Company: www.geese.co.uk.

The Medea Project: www.culturalodyssey.org/medea.

Only Connect: www.onlyconnectuk.org.

Pat Graney: www.patgraney.org.

People's Palace Projects: www.peoplespalace.org.uk.

Rideout: www.rideout.org.uk.

Synergy: www.synergytheatreproject.co.uk.

TiPP Centre: www.tipp.org.uk/tipp.

And this is a brief list of DVDs documenting specific theatre in prison projects:

Medea Project: Concrete Jungle. Dir. R. Jones. USA, 2006.

Mickey B. Dir. Tom Magill. Northern Ireland, 2008.

Shakespeare Behind Bars. Dir. H. Rogerson. USA, 2004.

We Just Telling Stories. Dir. L. Andrews. USA, 2001.

What I Want My Words to Do to You: Voices from inside a Women's Maximum Security Prison. Dir. J. Katz. USA, 2003.

index

acknowledgements

The author and publisher wish to thank the following for permission to reproduce copyright material:

For extracts from pp. 5–7 and pp. 39–40 from Caryl Churchill, *Softcops*, in *Plays Two*, Methuen (1990), © Caryl Churchill, *Softcops* and Methuen Drama, an imprint of A&C Black Publishers Ltd.

For extracts from p. 1 and pp. 52–54 from Tennessee Williams, *Not About Nightingales*, Methuen (1998), copyright © 1998 by The University of the South. Reprinted by permission of New Directions Publishing Corp and the Georges Borchardt Agency.

Many people have played a part in the development of this book. Thank you to Jen Harvie for your editorial care, perceptive comments and patience; to Kate Haines and Jenni Burnell at Palgrave Macmillan for your support and thoughtful feedback; to Paul Heritage and James Thompson for introducing me to the contradictory world of prisons and for sustaining conversations about them; to students at Goldsmiths and Queen Mary, University of London who have asked useful difficult questions about this field of work; to my colleagues at both institutions, particularly Sue Mayo, Cass Fleming, Katja Hilevaara and Catherine Silverstone, with whom I have had enjoyable and invaluable discussions about the book; and to Paul and Cora McAvinchey for their continuing interest and encouragement. This book is dedicated to David McFetridge, with love.